GREAT *American* GRILLING

The Ultimate Backyard Barbecue & Tailgating Cookbook

KENT WHITAKER

GREAT AMERICAN PUBLISHERS

WWW.GREATAMERICANPUBLISHERS.COM

TOLL-FREE 1.888.854.5954

Great American Publishers

501 Avalon Way, Suite B • Brandon, MS 39047
TOLL-FREE 1.888.854.5954
www.GreatAmericanPublishers.com

ISBN 978-1-934817-30-8

10 9 8 7 6 5 4 3 2

Designed by Cyndi Clark

Front cover image: istockphoto.com © gordana jovanovic • **Back cover food images:** © James Stefuik, www.carolinafoodphotography.com • **Back cover background:** istockphoto.com © Jag_cz • **Page food images** © James Stefuik, www.carolinafoodphotography.com: p25, p39, p52, p73, p85, p93, p111, p121, p130, p148, p187, p193, p207, p211, p221, p259, p275 • **Page 64**, Martinsville clock, Ridgeway Clocks www.ridgewayclocks.com • **Pages:** istockphoto.com © referenced by page number: p1, rgbdigital • p2, apomares • p4, maribee • p4, aopsan • p5, didecs • p6, Robert Ingelhart • p8, Big_Ryan • p8, Daniel R. Burch • p10, artisteer • p12, DimensionsDesigns • p12, Suzifoo • p12, DustyPixel • p12, ajafoto • p12, Diana Taliun • p14, jlvphoto • p14, Imagewriter • p15, alblec • p16, villorejo • p18, bhofack2 • p20, Pumpa1 • p20, Annetics • p23, DustyPixel • p24, ZU_09 • p27, Susan Trigg • p28, Lauri Patterson • p30, rimglow • p30, supermimicry • p30, Floortje • p30, studiocasper • p30, Floortje • p30, rimglow • p30, NYS444 • p31, caelmi • p33, wmaster890 • p35, STILLFX • p38, STILLFX • p41, AdShooter • p42, serkann007 • p43, Vrabelpeter1 • p42, mahmuttibet • p46, Nina Shannon • p46, Floortje • p47, YinYang • p48, Lauri Patterson • p50, StockImages_AT • p51, t: ShikharBhattarai • p51, rgbdigital • p54, William Mahar • p54, Kirby Hamilton • p55, aoshlick • p55, ultramarinfoto • p56, Floortje • p56, Olga Danylenko • p57, adlifemarketing • p58, Lauri Patterson • p61, Fisechko_Anastasia • p60, lenny777 • p62, Willard • p62, Anna Yu • p64, Popartic • p64, STILLFX • p66, George Manga • p68, EdnaM • p70, Catherine Lane • p74, t: DebbiSmirnoff • p77, Iryna Melnyk • p79, DustyPixel • p80, Suzifoo • p80, dehooks • p80, anna1311 • p80, nipapornnan • p81, Devonyu • p81, jesadaphorn • p83, karandaev • p86, ihoe • p87, ShikharBhattarai • p88, Aaron Nystrom • p89, Antagain • p89, Michael Phillips • p90, julichka • p91, Saddako • p95, 4kodiak • p97, Thomas Francois • p99, DebbiSmirnoff • p101, DebbiSmirnoff • p103, Donald Erickson • p105, lenny777 • p106, FarbaKolerova • p106, serguacom • p108, JohnnyMad • p114, Tatyana Nikitina • p115, LUHUANFENG • p117, jgroup • p119, karandaev • p120, Gudella • p120, Winai_Tepsuttinun • p122, minadezhda • p123, CSA-Archive • p124, CSA-Archive • p126, rimglow • p133, Zoediak • p135, 4kodiak • p136, tab1962 • p138, nicoolay • p140, Paul Cowan • p140, Lisovskaya • p142, mattjeacock • p144, naruedom • p147, p150, malerapaso • p151, Timeless889 • p155, mphillips007 • p156, MariuszBlach • p158, GOSPHOTODESIGN • p160, ifollowthe3way • p161, Olivier Blondeau • p163, Larry Rains • p165, 5PH • p168, evgenyb • p170, Kesu01 • p173, NI QIN • p176, mphillips007 • p179, 4kodiak • p180, perkmeup • p180, Coprid • p181, morningarage • p185, nicolebranan • p188, gbh007 • p190, luka lajst • p194, artJazz • p200, HandmadePictures • p202, ntstudio • p203, Edward ONeil Photography Inc. • p203, Cristian Baitg • p204, Oliver Hoffmann • p208, zhekos • p212, bonchan • p213, R9_RoNaLdO • p214, Lauri Patterson • p215, gemenacom • p218, Qanat Societa Cooperativa • p224, ajafoto • p226, AVNphotolab • p228, tubafirat • p230, ksushachmeister • p233, Natalie_B • p235, JackValley • p239, Ivenks • p242, Karim Hesham • p242, HandmadePictures • p250, Alena Dvorakova • p252, eli_asenova • p252, Viktor Lugovskoy • p252, Alexander Bryljaev • p252, 58shadows • p252, Tevarak • p252, urfinguss • p252, Nettedotca • p253, Iamthatiam • p255, Vitali Dyatchenko • p255, Lilyana Vynogradova • p256, hidesy • p258, DonNichols • p260, forcontrast • p262, DonNichols • p263, LeeAnnWhite • p264, MSPhotographic • p265, AndreaAstes • p267, milanfoto • p267, alex5248 • p267, FotografiaBasica • p267, FotografiaBasica • p267, FotografiaBasica • p267, mitchellpictures • p267, DipakShelare • p269, Yulia_Davidovich • p270, YinYang • p270, DustyPixel • p270, Coprid • p274, Vitalina Rybakova • p274, ajafoto

©Kent Whitaker or *provided by KW with credit on page: p7, p22, p23, *p34, *p38, p63, p65, p67, p68, p69, p69, p71, *p83, *p100, p129, p132, p134, *p152, p166, *p178, p183, p196, p205, p209, p217, p236, p238, p240, p243, p244, p245, p246, p248, p254, *p257, p268, p272, p273, p276, p286, Kent at the Grill

CONTENTS

INTRODUCTION

Can you smell the flavor? The United States has a deep love affair with grilling and barbecue. It's also been part of my family since I can remember. My grandparents in Alabama and Mississippi grilled over pecan, charcoal, and

My dad Eli Whitaker II

other woods. My dad mastered the art of campfire cooking and back yard grilling. Now, my brothers and I carry on the tradition by firing up the grill or smoker every chance we get.

My career in culinary writing and writing cookbooks began after I won the Emeril Live/Food Network Barbecue Contest. Since then my wife Ally, son Macee, and I have had the amazing opportunity to travel the country researching fantastic foods while working on new books, articles, and dishes.

In this book, I share with you 250 of my favorite recipes for grilling, barbecuing, and tailgating. It is my hope that if nothing else, you will have FUN cooking from my book, and, of course, cook some great food. A common theme in my writing is history, and this book is no exception. Throughout the book you will find fun history and trivia about the grilling and barbecue world I love so much.

Great American Grilling is dedicated to my wife Allyson and son Macee, as well as to all of the wonderful people who enjoy cooking outdoors. Nothing makes a meal taste better than enjoying it with family and friends!

TAILGATING TIPS

Tailgating at football games and NASCAR events has become a huge pastime and cottage industry. In fact, tailgating is not just for sports enthusiasts. Just ask any Jimmy Buffet fan. The bare-footed musician is known for his Trop-Rock tunes and devoted fans are nicknamed "parrot heads." Prior to each concert his fans turn parking lots into huge grilling parties. Here are a few things to keep in mind when tailgating, along with suggestions for keeping things safe. Look for this emblem throughout the book as suggestions for some great tailgate-friendly fare.

Before the Tailgate

- **Check the rules** for tailgating where you plan to have your big grilling party. They may not allow certain types of grills.

- **Inspect your grill**, smoker, and cooking items to ensure they are working.

- **Make sure you have plenty of fuel.** An extra tank of propane or bag of charcoal goes a long way.

- **If using charcoal**, make sure you have a way to properly extinguish your fire.

- **Do your prep work ahead of time.** Chopping, peeling, slicing, marinating, and even pre-cooking saves time at the tailgate. Make sure everything is stored properly at the right temperature until needed.

- **Invest in a meat thermometer** to ensure all meats are cooked properly.

- **Disposable is the way to go.** There's something to be said about not having to bring home a ton of dirty dishes to wash. Paper plates, plastic forks and spoons, and red Solo cups are very convenient for quick clean up. Bring along gallon-size zip-close bags and lidded plastic containers for any leftovers—and don't forget to pack a box of heavy-duty trash bags.

- **Pack extras.** You can always use extra plates, paper towels, napkins, plastic forks, and the like later. It's better to have too many than to run out.

- **Safety first!** A first aid kit is a great thing to take along in case of a minor mishap. Include bug spray, sunscreen, rain gear, and even some batteries and toilet paper.

Simple Starters

At the Tailgate

- **Control the temp.** Cold foods should be kept cold and hot foods should be kept hot. Sounds obvious, but remember—we don't want to send people to the ER.

- **Wash your hands.** Oh...And wash your hands again. Provide several containers of clean/sanitary wipes around your tailgate area for you and your guests.

- **Plan on using separate coolers** for meats, veggies and prepped foods, and ice for drinks. Always keep the ice you plan on using for drinking in a separate cooler from anything else. Even canned or bottled drinks should be kept separate from ice for drinks. Why? Think about it this way. Set your iced tea glass on a table and invite all of your friends to come by and stick their fingers in the glass before you have a sip. That reminds me...use an ice scoop.

- **Keep coolers** shaded and out of direct sunlight.

- **Cover everything.**

- **Avoid cross contamination** by keeping raw meat juices away from condiments, veggies, chips, and other items. Use separate cutting boards for meats, vegetables, and breads.

- **Hydrate!** Have plenty of water on hand. Bottled water in individual bottles and gallon containers are a must for tailgating on a hot day. A great way to keep drinks cold is to fill empty two liter soda bottles three quarters full with water and freeze. They turn into extra water as they melt.

- **When everything is served,** cover and properly store leftover items. Don't leave food items out for hours for people to walk by and grab a handful. Use common sense, a container of left-over mayo-based slaw needs to be properly stored and chilled long before the box of cookies you picked up at the store.

- **Check out other tailgaters** for ideas that fit into your budget and plans.

- **Oh, did I mention washing your hands?**

Sizzling
STARTERS

AWESOME APPETIZERS

Appetizer: A small dish of food or a drink taken before a meal or the main course of a meal to stimulate one's appetite.

source: Oxford Dictionaries

WHAT IS AN APPETIZER?

I noticed the word SMALL in the definition. If you drop by a many local restaurants, you'll notice the appetizer menu is packed with meal-sized portions. Over the years, it seems the meaning of appetizer has morphed into everything from finger foods to fine dining. When it comes to outdoor cooking, I agree that an appetizer can be just about anything...it's all a matter of portion size.

Smoked Sausage Puffs

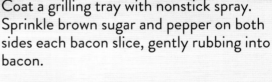

1 (16-ounce) package smoked
   sausage

½ cup chopped onion

½ cup chopped bell pepper

½ cup shredded Cheddar
   cheese

½ cup shredded mozzarella
   cheese

¼ cup mustard

Minced garlic

2 (8-ounce) cans crescent rolls

Cook smoked sausage
and finely chop or crumble.

Sauté veggies, if desired.

Mix all ingredients in a large bowl, except
crescents.

Coat a mini muffin pan with nonstick spray.
Break dough into small pieces and spread
pieces on a plate to stretch.

Place into muffin pan, spoon filling in and
fold edges over. Pinch to seal. Bake at 350°
until golden. Makes 24 to 30 puffs.

Candied Bacon

*A fun appetizer that is also delicious on a grilled cheeseburger. I suggest
using this with a charcoal grill because of the amount of grease.*

Bacon, sliced (thick or regular)

Brown sugar

Black pepper

Coat a grilling tray with nonstick spray.
Sprinkle brown sugar and pepper on both
sides each bacon slice, gently rubbing into
bacon.

For Grill: Grill over high heat (with a water
spray bottle on-hand for flare ups). Turn
gently as few times as possible.

For Oven: You can also cook in the oven
using a broiling rack and tray. The key is
allowing the fat to drain away as it cooks.

Texas Buffalo Eggs

Sure, the name sounds a bit goofy — I know buffalos don't lay eggs — however, this is one of those recipes that falls into both the appetizer and full meal categories, as you can make six appetizer-size portions or four mini-meatloaf-size portions.

4 to 6 small jalapeños

1 cup shredded pepper jack cheese (enough to stuff each pepper)

2 pounds ground beef

2 to 3 tablespoons steak sauce

⅓ cup minced onion

Salt and pepper to taste

Barbecue sauce

Cut tops off of each pepper, seed and rinse. Stuff each with jack cheese, loading it full.

In a bowl, combine ground beef, steak sauce, onion, salt and pepper. Mix well and divide into 4 or 6 equal portions.

On wax paper or a cookie sheet, press thin patties wide enough to wrap around each pepper to fully enclose it. You'll have several weird-looking, egg-shaped meatballs. Place in grill preheated to medium heat. Grill for several minutes to allow the beef to firm up before turning or gently rotating. Baste with barbecue sauce as you go.

You don't want to cook these too fast so that the pepper has time to cook and the cheese melts. On the other hand, don't overcook them because if cooked too long, the cheese could seep out.

Sizzling Starters

Wes' Spicy Grilled Jalapeño Canoes

It's a given. When we have a neighborhood grilling session, my buddy Wes will always show up with his signature grilled stuffed bacon and cheese jalapeños. Wes has perfected his jalapeño grilling technique to include specialized pepper holders for his grill. His best advice, use gloves to protect yourself when cleaning hot peppers. His second piece of advice, use real bacon bits or crumbled bacon. "The fake bacon bits just don't work as well," Wes says. "If you're going to go to all of the effort to clean a bunch of crazy hot peppers, then you might as well use some REAL bacon!" I can't argue with that. *Recipe courtesy of Wes Spencer*

Tailgate Friendly

20 to 24 jalapeños

2 (8-ounce) packages cream cheese, softened

1 (8-ounce) package finely shredded Cheddar cheese

1 (6-ounce) package of REAL bacon bits

NOT-SO-HOT: Swap the hot jalapeños for sweet and colorful mini peppers. If you still want just a little heat, add a little minced jalapeño or a few splashes of hot sauce.

Using latex or protective gloves, cut tops off jalapeños, cut peppers in half, remove seeds and white membrane and set aside on a large serving platter.

Place cream cheese in a mixing bowl. Using a large fork, mix in a little more than half the shredded cheese. Add bacon bits and mix well. Stuff pepper halves with mixture; level to the top of the halves.

For Grill: Coat or spray grill with oil, preheat to low heat and cook peppers 10 to 12 minutes, or until cheese is melted.

For Oven: Preheat oven to 325°. Place peppers on a treated cookie sheet about 1 inch apart. Heat 15 minutes or until cheese is melted.

Let stand 5 minutes and serve warm.

Stuffed Tomato Poppers

You'll enjoy the best of both worlds with this easy appetizer, as you can serve it chilled or hot, grilled or baked. It is best made with tomatoes slightly larger than a golf ball. The ingredients are simple, and you don't even need measurements – simply flavor it to your liking.

8 to 10 small tomatoes

1 cup shredded mozzarella cheese

1 cup crumbled feta cheese

¼ cup chopped fresh basil

¼ cup chopped green onions

1 teaspoon Italian seasoning

Olive oil

Balsamic vinaigrette, optional

Slice the tops off tomatoes and gently scoop out insides, being careful to not break the skin when scooping (discard pulp or reserve for a future recipe).

In a bowl, combine cheeses, basil, green onions, Italian seasoning and a small drizzle of olive oil. Toss to mix.

Fill each tomato with the cheese mixture. Serve chilled with a drizzle of balsamic vinaigrette applied just before serving.

TO SERVE HOT:

Place Stuffed Tomato Poppers on a medium-hot grill or in oven at 350° and cook 8 to 10 minutes. (Be careful not to overcook or they become too fragile to handle.)

Mini Cream Cheese Calzone Poppers

Yep, you can grill up a batch of mini calzones and serve them up as appetizers. The great thing is that you can make any flavor calzone you enjoy. For instance, you may choose shrimp to complement your grilled seafood dinner.

2 (12-ounce) cans refrigerated
  biscuits

Cream cheese, softened

Pizza sauce

Italian seasoning

Your choice of meat topping

Shredded cheese

Preheat grill to medium-high heat. Use the upper rack (if possible) with a grilling tray.

Open the cans of biscuits and flatten each biscuit to as wide as you can get it without breaking. They will pull back slightly. Work in small portions.

Add a bit of cream cheese spread across the dough and cover the cream cheese with pizza sauce. Then add a dash of Italian seasoning. Add your choice of meat and some cheese to one side of the dough. Fold dough over and pinch to close.

Place evenly on a grilling tray prepped with nonstick spray, if needed. Place on the upper rack of your preheated grill and close the cover. Allow the grill to work as an oven to cook evenly. Serve hot when dough is slightly golden.

FOR MINI PIZZAS:

Center ingredients on dough and leave dough flat for mini pizzas.

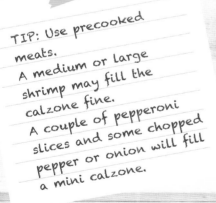

TIP: Use precooked meats.
A medium or large shrimp may fill the calzone fine.
A couple of pepperoni slices and some chopped pepper or onion will fill a mini calzone.

President and Laura Bush's Deviled Eggs

President Bush and his wife Laura added their recipe for Deviled Eggs to a collection of dishes offered up to the nation heading into the 2004 Fourth of July holiday. The recipe even included a note from the first family about their choice of hot sauce.

12 large eggs, hard-boiled and peeled

1 tablespoon (plus) soft butter

1 tablespoon (plus) mayonnaise

1 tablespoon Dijon mustard

½ teaspoon Yucatan Sunshine Habanero sauce

Salt to taste

Paprika, for garnish

Chopped parsley, for garnish

Cut eggs in half, remove yolks and set aside the whites.

Put egg yolks in a food processor and add remaining ingredients, except garnish. Process 20 seconds or until blended. Check for taste and increase mustard, salt or Habanero sauce, if desired.

Place mixture in a piping bag with star tip and pipe into egg halves. Sprinkle with paprika and chopped parsley. Chill for about an hour before serving.

Yucatan Sunshine Habanero sauce can be substituted with Tabasco sauce. The Bushes used Yucatan Sunshine Habanero when living in Texas. When they lived in the White House, the White House chef used the sauce in a variety of recipes.

Recipe - Georgewbush-whitehouse.archives.gov

Customize your Deviled Eggs

Are you a bit bored with your standard Deviled Egg recipe? Then it's time to give your boring eggs a facelift. Here are a few ideas on making a simple recipe your own signature dish that will have people coming back for more.

FANCY DEVILED EGGS:

What's the difference between "fancy" and plain ole' Deviled Eggs? Not much, except a few changes.

- Switch mustard to Dijon mustard.
- Add a tablespoon of minced celery (or onion or bell pepper).
- Add a bit of sour cream or salad dressing for part (or all) of the mayonnaise.

SEAFOOD DEVILED EGGS:

Use your favorite Deviled Egg recipe and go the seafood route.

- Add 2 to 3 tablespoons chopped salad shrimp or broken crabmeat.
- Add 2 to 3 teaspoons seafood seasoning.

FUN ADDITIONS:

Here's a list of added ingredients that you can toss in the bowl when making Deviled Eggs. Choose one or as many as you like.

- Bacon bits
- Chopped jalapeños
- Swap sweet relish with sweet jalapeño relish
- Shredded cheese
- Pimento cheese
- Chopped olives
- Mashed avocados
- Cream cheese or flavored cream cheese spread
- Dash of barbecue sauce, or hot sauce, or Duck Sauce, or Italian dressing...
- Chopped chicken
- The sky is the limit!

Mary's Grilled Ham and Pickle Rollups

My friend Marv has recently become addicted to an appetizer his mother in law, Mary Chitester of Grant, Alabama, prepares. Marv says, "The combination of sweet and sour, along with a cold beverage, makes for a perfect pre-meal treat while you get your grill going. I've made these appetizers all summer long each time I grill," Marv said of his mother-in-law's recipe. The great thing is the recipe can be made all year long. Prepare some for a summer cookout or a winter holiday party.

Ingredients	Instructions
1 (8-ounce) package cream cheese, softened	Allow cream cheese to warm to near room temperature.
12 to 14 ham slices	Lay ham slices out, spread cream cheese over slice, add a slice of pickle and roll up. Cut into equal segments (1 inch or so), and secure with a toothpick.
12 to 14 crispy dill pickles	
Toothpicks	
	Place on your grill just long enough to warm ham. And, they are great served cold!

Prosciutto-Wrapped Grilled Peaches

4 firm ripe peaches, peeled and quartered

16 slices prosciutto (narrow slices work best)

½ to 1 cup brown sugar

Wrap each peach quarter with prosciutto and secure with a toothpick. Sprinkle lightly with brown sugar. Place on a grill preheated to medium-high heat and cook 4 to 6 minutes just until grill marks appear (do not overcook as peaches will become mushy).

Grilled Pineapple Rings

This recipe makes a great appetizer because it's not too heavy and so filling that no one will want to dive into the main course. The perfect accompaniment for just about any grilled seafood, pork tenderloin, pork chops, and assorted other meats. You can substitute well-drained canned pineapple in a pinch.

1 pineapple, peeled, cored and cut into rings

3 tablespoons melted butter or margarine

½ cup brown sugar

Brush pineapple rings with butter and place on a preheated medium-high grill. (The grates need to be hot enough to leave grill marks.) After flipping them the first time, sprinkle the cooked side with brown sugar to coat evenly.

Cut into bite-size pieces and serve hot with toothpicks and your favorite yogurt dipping sauce.

GRILL TALK: You can use rings or large chunks, toothpicks or skewers. Grilled pineapples, and other grilled fruits, make great desserts as well as fantastic appetizers during hot summer months.

Loaded Jalapeño Potato Skins

You can use whole potatoes purchased especially for this recipe or save the skins from a batch of mashed potatoes or potato salad. There's nothing like a little recycling.

Tailgate Friendly

6 large baking potatoes, baked

½ stick butter, melted

Salt and pepper to taste

1 onion, finely chopped

2 to 3 tablespoons minced jalapeño

⅓ cup bacon bits (or cooked and crumbled bacon)

⅔ cup shredded Cheddar cheese

Sour cream for topping or dipping

Preheat grill to medium hot. Slice potatoes in half and scoop out the middle, leaving a nice layer of potato on the skin.

Brush each skin with melted butter on both sides; season with salt and pepper. Microwave on high about 5 minutes to start the cooking process.

Place skins open side down in a grilling basket prepped with nonstick spray and grill about 5 minutes until edges are golden. Turn skins over and start loading them down with onion, jalapeño, bacon and cheese (or any extra items that you desire); don't use all your cheese.

Continue to grill the potatoes 7 to 10 minutes until heated through. Top with remaining cheese and grill until cheese melts. Serve hot with sour cream.

Sizzling Starters

Cheesy Barbecue Stuffed Mushrooms

8 medium (or 4 large) mushroom caps

¼ cup butter

⅓ cup chopped onion

¼ cup chopped green bell pepper

¼ cup chopped red bell pepper

½ cup pulled pork chopped into small pieces

2 to 3 tablespoons barbecue sauce

⅔ cup mixed shredded cheese

2 tablespoons mayonnaise or cream cheese

Salt and pepper to taste

Wash and pat mushrooms dry with paper towels. Remove stems, chop and set aside.

Melt butter in a skillet over medium-high heat. Add onion, peppers and chopped stems. Sauté until onion is translucent and peppers are softened. Remove to a bowl and allow it to cool slightly.

Add barbecue sauce, cheese, mayonnaise, salt and pepper. Mix well and spoon into mushroom caps.

Grill over medium-high heat using a grilling tray or basket on the upper shelf for 7 to 10 minutes until heated through and cheese is melted.

EASY BACON-WRAPPED STUFFED MUSHROOMS:

This is more of a food hack than a recipe. Get some prepackaged stuffed mushrooms. Wrap them in bacon slices, secure with a toothpick, sprinkle with your favorite seasoning or rub and grill until hot.

Awesome Appetizers

Rooster Sauce Bacon-Wrapped Onion Rings

I love this recipe! I saw some guys grilling these at a tailgate and had to try them. A slick onion slice coated in sauce and wrapped in slippery bacon can be a bit hard to handle, but the payoff is worth the effort. And if you're wondering what "Rooster Sauce" is, simply look for the bottle of hot sauce at the store with the green cap and the huge rooster logo.

4 to 5 large sweet onions

½ cup Rooster Sauce (Sriracha hot chili sauce)

2 tablespoons mayonnaise

Dash soy sauce

Dash lemon or lime juice

1 (16-ounce) package bacon

1 tablespoon brown sugar

½ tablespoon black pepper

Cut onions into ½-inch thick slices. Separate into rings using only larger rings.

In a large bowl, combine Rooster Sauce, mayonnaise, soy sauce and lemon juice.

Separate bacon slices and gently stir into sauce to coat. Wrap each onion slice with bacon (wrapping the bacon all the way around the ring; it may take more than one piece of bacon); secure with a toothpick.

Brush remaining sauce over rings and sprinkle with brown sugar and black pepper.

Use a grilling basket or tray and grill slowly over a medium grill (about 250° to 350°) about an hour or until bacon is brown.

GRILL TALK: Feel free to use flavored or thick-cut bacon. When grilling or baking, be sure to use a drip pan and rack. The bacon firms up better when the grease is allowed to drip away.

Sizzling Starters

Vegetable Cream Cheese Pizza

This versatile recipe has become a favorite over the years because it's easy to prepare and the options are endless. I suggest starting with your favorite cream cheese spread flavor. Also, thoroughly drain excess moisture from vegetables like cucumber slices and tomatoes so your cream cheese and crust do not become soggy.

Tailgate Friendly

1 (14-ounce) can refrigerated pizza dough

½ cup flavored cream cheese spread

2 to 3 tablespoons sour cream, optional

1 teaspoon dried dill

1 teaspoon celery powder

1 teaspoon garlic powder

Assorted fresh vegetables

Preheat oven according to directions on pizza dough package and cook pizza dough into a crust as described. Cool completely.

In small bowl, combine cream cheese, sour cream, dill, celery powder and garlic powder. Mix until smooth and spread evenly over crust.

Top with vegetables. Serve immediately, or cover and keep chilled until serving.

Cut into equal bite-sized portions and place on a serving dish as an appetizer.

TOPPING SUGGESTIONS:
- Crumbled broccoli florets
- Cucumber slices
- Diced tomato
- Chopped red onions
- Sliced olives
- Shredded carrots

Sizzling Starters

Asian-Style Chicken Lettuce Wrap Appetizers

CHICKEN:

½ cup cashews, whole or pieces

¼ cup unsalted sunflower seeds

1 head butter lettuce

1 small sweet onion, finely chopped

1 small carrot, sliced

2 tablespoons butter, optional

1 pound chicken, cooked and chopped

1 (8-ounce) can sliced water chestnuts

1 tablespoon minced garlic

1½ tablespoons soy sauce

½ tablespoon rice vinegar

½ cup cooked rice (more if you need to feed a few more people)

ASIAN FINISHING SAUCE:

⅔ cup Asian sweet chili sauce

½ tablespoon lime juice

1 tablespoon chopped fresh cilantro

1 tablespoon hoisin sauce

Lightly toast cashews and sunflower seeds on separate cookie sheets in 300° oven. Cook 5 to 7 minutes until lightly toasted; sunflower seeds will cook fastest. Watch carefully so they don't burn.

Gently break off lettuce leaves, rinse and allow to dry.

Sauté onion and carrot in 2 tablespoons butter, if desired. Combine with cashews, sunflower seeds, chicken and remaining ingredients in a foil pan. Stir to mix well, cover with foil, and place on a medium-high preheated grill. Grill about 20 minutes or until heated through.

For Finishing Sauce: Combine ingredients in a small bowl; mix well. Serve alongside chicken filling and lettuce, allowing your guests to fill their own lettuce cups and drizzle with sauce.

TOTALLY CHEATING:
Short on time? My tailgate buddy says: "Grab a few cans or frozen family-style Chinese dinners from the store. Toss in extras like cooked chicken, fresh veggies, etc. Heat and serve with your lettuce wraps."

Mini Creamy Cucumber and Onion Tea-Party Sandwiches

If you've worked all summer in your garden and all you have is a basketful of cucumbers that the squirrels didn't chew on, then I have a solution. Why not whip up a batch of quick and easy cucumber tea-party sandwiches? If you can't find a Vidalia onion then substitute it with another variety of sweet onion. Call these Mini Creamy Cucumber and Vidalia Onion Tea-Party Sandwiches for a nice summer gathering, or call them Cucumber and Onion Sliders for your next tailgate party.

1 large cucumber

1 (8-ounce) package cream cheese, softened

2½ tablespoons sour cream

1½ tablespoons finely chopped Vidalia onion

1½ tablespoons Dijon mustard

1 tablespoon minced celery

1 tablespoon minced carrot

⅓ cup almond slices, toasted

Salt and pepper to taste

Dash fennel

Dash parsley flakes

Mini loaf bread (rye if you can find it)

Peel cucumber and remove and discard seeds. Grate cucumber and place in a colander to drain. To ensure it is completely dry, squeeze cucumber in a paper-towel.

Combine remaining ingredients, except bread, in a bowl; mix well. Add cucumber to cream cheese mixture; mix well.

Refrigerate at least 1 hour or until ready to serve. Spread mixture evenly over bread to make miniature sandwiches...or sliders.

Sizzling Starters

Gramp's Nuts, Bolts and Screws

My grandmother Harriett Whitaker of Grenada, Mississippi, made this for my Gramp, Eli Whitaker Senior. It is her version of the classic holiday mix and makes a large amount (it can be halved). Gramp called this his "nuts, bolts and screws."

2 sticks butter

3 tablespoons Worcestershire sauce

2 tablespoons each: garlic salt, onion powder, celery salt

2 teaspoons hot sauce

1 (14-ounce) box Wheat Chex cereal

1 (12-ounce) box Rice Chex cereal

1 (8-ounce) bag pretzel sticks

2 cups Cheerios cereal

1 cup chopped pecans

Melt butter in a saucepan. Add Worcestershire, garlic salt, onion powder, celery salt and hot sauce.

In a large bowl, combine butter sauce and remaining ingredients. Stir to mix well.

Heat oven to 225° and spread mixture over 3 cookie sheets.

Bake 1½ hours while turning often with a spoon. Bake just until crisp, being careful not to burn.

Cool slightly before serving.

Man Cave Mixed Nuts

I made this quick and easy appetizer when faced with a time crunch and limited supplies.

1 (15-ounce) can mixed nuts

½ stick butter, melted

1 tablespoon brown sugar

Dash hot sauce

Dash chili powder

Preheat grill or oven to 300°. Mix all ingredients, stirring to evenly coat nuts. Spread evenly over a cookie sheet.

Grill about 20 minutes or until heated through. Use an indirect grilling method and keep the lid closed.

Cool slightly before serving.

LET'S GET DIPPING

DIP OVERHAUL

Have you ever been to a cookout that didn't offer assorted dips and chips? There's nothing wrong with some good old store-bought French onion dip or a jar of salsa if you're in a time crunch. But don't your chips, crackers and veggie tray deserve better? Instead of the normal tub or bowl of your typical dip options, I think it's time to bring a little culinary life to the world of dips, salsa, and more.

Creamy Vidalia Onion and Bacon Dip

If you ask me, there's no better onion out there than a Vidalia onion. The flavor is perfect for making onion dip.

1 tablespoon olive oil

2 Vidalia onions, chopped

Salt and pepper to taste

⅓ cup real bacon bits (small bits, not large chunks)

1½ teaspoons sugar

1 cup sour cream

2 to 3 ounces cream cheese, softened

1½ teaspoons white wine vinegar

Chopped parsley

Heat oil over medium heat in a saucepan or skillet. Add onions, salt and pepper; cook until onions are brown but not burned.

Remove from heat and pour into a bowl to cool completely.

Add remaining ingredients and mix well. Cover and chill at least 1 hour or until ready to serve.

Almond Onion Spinach Dip

The trick to this recipe is starting early to thaw the spinach.

1 (10-ounce) package frozen chopped spinach

1 (16-ounce) carton sour cream

1 (8-ounce) package cream cheese, softened

2 teaspoons Dijon mustard

1 (1.9-ounce) envelope instant onion soup mix

½ cup chopped almonds

¼ cup chopped onion

1 teaspoon minced garlic

Dash salt and pepper

Dash Worcestershire sauce

Completely thaw spinach and drain at least 5 minutes. Squeeze spinach in a paper towel to remove any remaining moisture and chop slightly.

Combine with remaining ingredients in a bowl and mix well. Cover and chill before serving.

Just Plain Lazy Bacon Spinach Dip

Here's a way to fake a great tasting spinach dip in minutes. It's either a really impressive recipe hack or just plain lazy.

1 (10-ounce) package frozen chopped spinach, thawed and drained

1 (15-ounce) jar creamy ranch dip

½ cup mayonnaise or sour cream

¼ cup real bacon bits

Combine all in a bowl, cover, chill and serve. Too easy!

Sizzling Starters

First Lady Laura Bush's Guacamole

First Lady Laura Bush brought her recipe for Guacamole to the table when asked for recipes to include on the White House website. The collection of recipes was posted prior to the Fourth of July 2004 and included dishes from her husband, President George W. Bush, as well as members of his staff, including Secretary Ashcroft.

8 ripe avocados

4 lemons, juiced

7 shallots, finely chopped

1 jalapeño, seeded and finely chopped

½ bunch cilantro, finely chopped

1 teaspoon black pepper

1 tablespoon salt

Halve and pit avocados and scoop flesh into a bowl. Mash to desired consistency and mix in remaining ingredients.

Cover with plastic wrap and refrigerate for about an hour before serving. Serve with tortilla chips.

Recipe courtesy of Georgewbush-whitehouse.archives.gov

Tailgate Friendly

Let's Get Dipping

Mexican Restaurant Style White Cheese Dip

Have you ever tried to make your own White Cheese Dip and come up short on texture and flavor? How do you solve the mystery of how it's made? Ask the cook at a Mexican restaurant. It turns out that cheese dip is actually more of a cheese sauce. Use white American cheese from your local deli and don't have them slice it.

1 pound white American deli cheese, cubed

1 cup milk or half-and-half

2 tablespoons diced jalapeño

1 teaspoon cumin

1 teaspoon chili powder

¼ teaspoon salt

¼ teaspoon black pepper

Use a double boiler (or a saucepan as long as you cook using low heat). Add cheese and about half the milk. As cheese melts, add additional milk to your desired consistency.

Add remaining ingredients, stir and serve warm.

LBJ LOVED BARBECUES AND GRILLING

President Lyndon B. Johnson, or LBJ as he was commonly call, was known for his love of barbecue and grilling. The White House, and his Ranch, were host to many dinners that often featured Texas style cooking, barbecue, or massive grilling sessions. Pictured here in April of 1967 are several Latin American ambassadors enjoying a barbecue at the LBJ Ranch. The event even included a mariachi band from Brownsville, Texas.

Source: Library of Congress / LBJ Presidential Library

Sizzling Starters

Lysa's Homemade Salsa

My friend Lysa Burns-Brown has tried every recipe for salsa that she can find, and used that expertise to perfect her own homemade salsa. She shared it with me years ago and I'm sharing it with you now.

6 to 8 fresh tomatoes, chopped, divided

1 green bell pepper, chopped

½ red bell pepper, chopped

1 orange bell pepper, chopped

2 small red chile peppers, chopped

⅛ small habanero pepper, chopped

3 to 4 jalapeños, chopped

1 sweet yellow onion, chopped

⅓ bunch cilantro, chopped

1 teaspoon salt

Juice of 1 lime

Set aside half the chopped tomatoes in a separate bowl.

Place half the chopped tomatoes in a food processor along with remaining ingredients, except salt and lime. Pulse until chopped to desired consistency.

Add salt and lime juice and pulse until well blended (5 to 7 seconds).

Pour into a large bowl with remaining half of chopped tomatoes and stir, making sure to blend together thoroughly. Chill 3 hours.

Pour into sterilized jars—the kind used for canning, and keep chilled. Serve with chips suitable for dipping.

SALSA!

Beginning in 1992, salsa outsells ketchup in United States grocery stores. Salsa, the Italian and Spanish term for sauce, can be used as a dip, condiment or cooking sauce. While ingredients will vary from country to country, for most people living in the United States, salsa refers to the chunky tomato-based sauces popular in Mexican and Tex-Mex cuisine. However, varieties of salsa range from mild to extremely hot to those made with fruit.

Quick and Easy Salsa

2 cups chopped tomatoes

⅓ cup chopped onion

1½ tablespoons chopped cilantro

2 tablespoons lime juice

1 tablespoon chopped jalapeño

Dash chili powder

Dash salt and pepper

Combine all ingredients in a bowl, cover and chill before serving.

QUICK AND EASY FRUIT SALSA:

Start with the basic recipe for Quick and Easy Salsa and replace one cup tomatoes with a cup of chopped fresh fruit—peaches, nectarines, mangoes, pineapple or a mix. Heck, you can even use a can of mixed fruit.

SALSA SAFE! Salsa is a staple for tailgating and backyard grilling. However, many people don't realize that this tasty dish needs to be properly stored and chilled.

Creamy Cucumber Dip

1 large cucumber

¾ cup plain yogurt

¾ cup sour cream

2 tablespoons olive oil

4 teaspoons minced fresh dill

2 teaspoons red wine vinegar

2 to 3 teaspoons minced garlic

1 teaspoon Worcestershire sauce

Parsley flakes

Peel cucumber and cut it in half lengthwise. Use a spoon to scoop out seeds and discard them. Finely chop the cucumber and drain on paper towels several minutes (otherwise, your dip will be too runny).

Combine drained cucumber and remaining ingredients in a bowl. Mix well and chill before serving.

Sizzling Starters

Cajun Chicken Dip

My good friends down in the Delta, Toby and Lamar Bertrand, shared this recipe with me several years ago. Their family business, Landry's Pepper Company, has been growing peppers and making premium hot sauces for more than seven generations. The Bertrand family lost Toby this year and I decided to dust off this recipe as a tribute to a great guy and his wonderful wife, Lamar.

1 stick butter

1 small onion, chopped

1 bell pepper, chopped

1 (10.75-ounce) can cream of mushroom soup

1 cup chopped cooked chicken

½ tablespoon Cajun seasoning (Creole seasoning for less heat)

2 tablespoons sour cream

1 tablespoon Landry Pepper Hot Sauce (or your favorite)

Melt butter in a saucepan over medium heat; add onion and bell pepper and cook until clear.

Add mushroom soup and chicken and stir. Add remaining ingredients and mix well. Continue to cook until heated through, 5 to 7 minutes.

Serve hot in a chafing dish with Fritos or party crackers.

Let's Get Dipping

Creamy Salmon Dip

My sister-in-law, Tonya, introduced me to salmon dip with this fantastic recipe. It's easy to prepare and is always a party pleaser.

1 (14-ounce) can red salmon, drained

⅓ cup light cream

2 (3-ounce) packages cream cheese, softened

¼ cup lemon juice

1 tablespoon dill weed

1 tablespoon parsley

1 teaspoon minced onion

½ teaspoon minced garlic

Large dash celery salt

Salt and pepper to taste

Combine all ingredients in a bowl and mix until smooth. Cover and refrigerate until ready to serve.

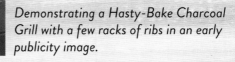

THE ORIGINAL HASTY BAKE CHARCOAL GRILL!

In 1948, Grant Hastings produced the first Hasty-Bake Charcoal Oven. As one of the original manufacturers of the "backyard barbecue," Hastings was a pioneer in the industry. Specifically, Hasty-Bake introduced the first portable unit, the first hooded unit, and a new method of cooking using indirect heat. Hastings' design controlled the intensity of heat by using vents, a heat deflector, a vent-less hood and an adjustable fire box, revolutionizing the method in which food was cooked. Today the grills are still made by hand in the USA at the company's headquarters in Tulsa, Oklahoma.

Photo courtesy of Hasty-Bake Charcoal Grills

Demonstrating a Hasty-Bake Charcoal Grill with a few racks of ribs in an early publicity image.

Sizzling Starters

Chocolate Coconut Cream Dip

1 (8-ounce) carton whipped topping (not canned)

1 to 2 tablespoons chocolate syrup

¼ cup coconut flakes, toasted

Thaw whipped topping and stir in chocolate syrup; mix well. Top with toasted coconut flakes, and serve with your favorite fruit for dipping.

You can't beat a great fruit dip on a sunny spring day. These quick and easy recipes are a great addition to any cookout or party. Use with fruit of all types or even assorted veggies and more.

Honey Yogurt Fruit Dip

2 (8-ounce) cartons flavored yogurt

¼ cup honey

Dash ground cinnamon

Mix all ingredients together, cover and chill before serving. Serve with assorted fruit.

Peanut Butter Yogurt Dip

2 to 3 tablespoons peanut butter

2 (8-ounce) cartons vanilla or chocolate yogurt

1 tablespoon dark brown sugar

Put peanut butter in a bowl and add a spoonful of yogurt to soften it. Continue adding yogurt a little at a time, mixing well after each addition, until you have the yogurt fully incorporated.

Add brown sugar and mix well. Cover and chill before serving. Serve with fruit, veggies or chips. Let me tell you...this dip is great with pretzels.

Sizzling Starters

TNGA Apple Caramel Dip

Ally and I love visiting our east Tennessee mountains and the north Georgia mountains every fall in search of apples and apple festivals. This dip recipe is perfect for fall tailgate grilling when fresh apples are plentiful. It's named in honor of a small town located on the state line of Tennessee and Georgia.

1 (8-ounce) package cream cheese, softened

¾ cup brown sugar

1 (8-ounce) carton sour cream

2 teaspoons vanilla extract

Squirt of lemon juice

1 cup cold milk

1 (3.4-ounce) box vanilla instant pudding mix

In a mixing bowl, combine cream cheese and brown sugar; mix until smooth.

Add sour cream, vanilla, lemon juice, milk and pudding mix.

Mix well, chill and serve with freshly cut apples, assorted fruit and even with grilled apples.

GRILLED SANDWICHES

SANDWICH GRILLING TIPS

- Always preheat your grill.
- Use the upper rack if possible. Or, start on the grill grates and move the sandwich to an upper rack to finish.
- Use a grilling tray, basket or thick foil.
- Precook greasy meats to allow excess fat from soaking your bread, as well as ensuring the meat is fully cooked.
- Hearty bread, rolls and buns stand up better to the grilling process than slices of delicate white bread.
- Be sure to clean and oil the grill grates – or use nonstick spray – when not using a grilling basket. Oh, don't forget to prep the basket as well.
- Many times the pieces of sandwich can be grilled separately and assembled on the grill.

Texas Toast Grilled Pepper Jack Cheese & Jalapeño Sandwich

Going big on the bread, such as thick slices of Texas Toast, is a no brainer for me when it comes to grilled cheese sandwiches cooked on an actual grill. This recipe is for one sandwich, but you can simply adjust the ingredients according to how many you need to make.

Tailgate Friendly

2 slices Texas toast

Butter or butter spray

2 pepper jack cheese slices

3 to 5 jalapeño slices (out of a jar)

2 thin onion slices

1 thin red bell pepper slice

⅛ cup sour cream

Preheat grill to medium low and coat clean grates with oil or nonstick spray (or use a treated grilling basket or tray).

Coat 1 side of each piece of toast with butter. Place 1 piece, butter-side-down, on grate. Add a slice of cheese, jalapeños, onions and bell pepper.

Top with another slice of cheese then remaining piece of Texas toast, butter-side-up. Turn once or twice until golden brown and cheese has melted. Serve hot with sour cream on the side for dipping.

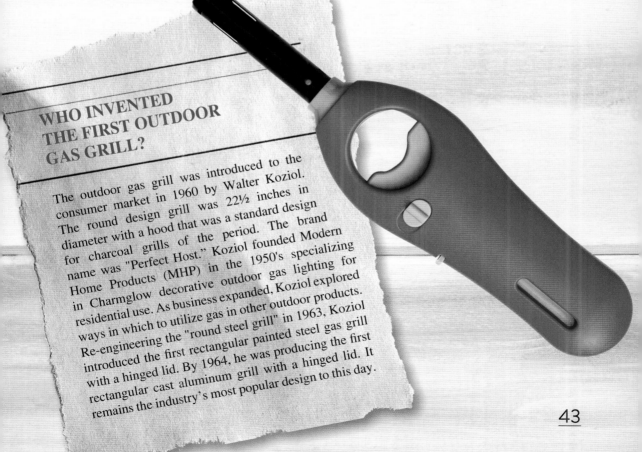

WHO INVENTED THE FIRST OUTDOOR GAS GRILL?

The outdoor gas grill was introduced to the consumer market in 1960 by Walter Koziol. The round design grill was 22½ inches in diameter with a hood that was a standard design for charcoal grills of the period. The brand name was "Perfect Host." Koziol founded Modern Home Products (MHP) in the 1950's specializing in Charmglow decorative outdoor gas lighting for residential use. As business expanded, Koziol explored ways in which to utilize gas in other outdoor products. Re-engineering the "round steel grill" in 1963, Koziol introduced the first rectangular painted steel gas grill with a hinged lid. By 1964, he was producing the first rectangular cast aluminum grill with a hinged lid. It remains the industry's most popular design to this day.

Grilled Pimento Cheese Sandwich

My buddy Wes is a "pimento cheese snob." In fact, so is my wife Allyson! Wes' pimento cheese recipe turned into a grilled delight. Wes is very specific with the ingredients to use for the best flavor, saying, "Use New York-style extra sharp cheese. Not just sharp, not just extra sharp, but New York extra sharp. Don't skimp on cheap pimentos; buy the good ones. If at all possible, it must be Duke's brand mayonnaise.

WES' PIMENTO CHEESE:

- 1 (1-pound) block New York-style extra sharp cheese
- 1 (4-ounce) jar pimentos
- 1 (16-ounce) jar Duke's mayonnaise
- Salt and pepper to taste

Shred cheese into a bowl with a lid. Add about half each of pimento and mayo; mix well. Add salt and pepper to taste. Add more mayonnaise and pimentos to your taste. Cover and chill 2 hours before using.

SANDWICH:

- Ciabatta rolls, hearty fresh deli rolls or French bread
- Butter
- Wes's Pimento Cheese

For Sandwich: Spread bread with butter and place on grill to heat and give some proper grill marks.

Spoon pimento cheese onto bottom of rolls. Add top rolls and move sandwich to top rack (or cooler place on grill). Continue to grill until rolls are golden and Wes's Pimento Cheese is beginning to melt. Serve immediately.

You can cook using a grill basket or layer of foil if needed. Or, wrap the sandwich completely in foil and place over indirect heat for a hot and tasty gooey delight worthy of eating with a fork.

Hoagie-Style Three-Cheese Grilled Ham & Cheese Sandwich with Raspberry Barbecue Sauce

When planning your grocery list, make sure you pick up enough cheese and ham. For each sandwich consider one or two slices of each cheese, as well as several slices of ham. This may differ depending on the size of your hoagie rolls. For instance, smaller slider-style hoagie buns only need one, or less, slices of each cheese per sandwich. A full-size roll will handle two slices of each cheese per sandwich.

2 hoagie buns

Butter or butter spray

1 to 2 Swiss cheese slices

1 to 2 Asiago cheese slices

1 to 2 Cheddar cheese slices

3 to 4 ham slices

RASPBERRY BARBECUE SAUCE:

1 cup ketchup

1 small jar raspberry jam (jelly or preserves work, too)

½ cup water

¼ cup apple cider vinegar

2 tablespoons yellow mustard

1½ tablespoons brown sugar

1 tablespoon onion powder (not onion salt)

½ tablespoon garlic powder (not garlic salt)

Dash liquid smoke

Preheat grill to medium hot. Split buns and spread insides with butter. Place on grate with inside of bun facing down, until hot.

Working quickly, flip buns and add cheese slices and ham to bottom of bun. Place top bun and continue grilling until cheese is melted. Serve with Raspberry Barbecue Sauce for dipping.

For Sauce: Combine all ingredients in a saucepan over low heat and cook until raspberry jam is melted and all ingredients are well mixed.

GRILL TALK: The Raspberry Barbecue Sauce is also perfect for other dishes. Consider using it with burgers, hot dogs, sausages, chicken, and more. It's also pretty awesome for a slow cooker full of meatballs!

Pita Gyros with Cucumber Sauce

If you enjoy the taste of a gyro with cucumber sauce, then there's no reason why you shouldn't try a grilled version. You choose the meat of your choice — lamb, steak, chicken or a combo of your favorites.

CUCUMBER SAUCE:

1 cup plain yogurt

1 tablespoon mayonnaise

⅓ cup minced cucumber, about half a cucumber

1 tablespoon extra virgin olive oil

1½ teaspoons fresh lemon juice

Salt and pepper to taste

MEAT AND MARINADE:

3 tablespoons extra virgin olive oil

3 tablespoons fresh lemon juice

1 tablespoon oregano

½ tablespoon minced garlic

2 teaspoons salt

2 teaspoons ground black pepper

1½ pounds meat of your choice, thinly sliced

FINISHING:

½ onion, thinly sliced

1 (6-count) package pita pocket bread, halved

1 tomato, chopped, sliced or wedge cut

¼ head lettuce, shredded

For Cucumber Sauce: Combine all ingredients in a bowl and mix well. Cover and chill. (You can use a food processor to mince the cucumber.)

For Meat and Marinade: Mix marinade ingredients together and add meat. Toss and stir to coat pieces evenly; chill overnight.

Finishing: Place meat and onion in a grilling basket or tray on grill preheated to medium high. Grill about 10 minutes or until fully cooked, turning as needed. While meat is finishing on grill you can heat pita pockets, if desired. Stuff pita pockets with meat, tomatoes and lettuce; top with sauce. Serve quickly while hot.

Sizzling Starters

Cajun Chicken Cobb Salad Wrap

Ok, this recipe does not finish up on the grill, but it does start there!

1½ pounds chicken tenders or boneless chicken

Olive oil

Cajun seasoning

½ cup chopped sweet onion

1 tomato, chopped

2 hard-boiled eggs, chopped

1 (11-ounce) can whole-kernel corn, drained

¼ cup red wine vinegar

1 tablespoon olive oil

½ tablespoon Dijon mustard

1 teaspoon sugar

Salt and pepper to taste

12 small flour tortillas

½ head lettuce, shredded

Blue cheese, crumbled

Baste chicken tenders with olive oil and sprinkle with Cajun seasoning to taste.

Grill over medium-high heat, turning as needed, until juices run clear. While chicken is cooking, go ahead prepare the rest of the recipe.

In a medium bowl, combine onion, tomato, eggs and corn. Toss to mix. Add vinegar, olive oil, mustard, sugar, salt and pepper. Stir gently.

Top each tortilla with some shredded lettuce, vegetable mix, grilled chicken and blue cheese to taste. Roll and serve.

Foot-Long Tri-Tip Steak Sandwiches

For some backyard grillers the tri-tip steak may be somewhat of a mystery. For the best results, marinate meat overnight, cook it low and slow and slice across the grain.

1 pound tri-tip steak, roast cut

1 (12-ounce) can beer

2 cups steak sauce, divided

Your favorite rub, seasoning or steak seasoning

1 stick butter, melted, divided

1 onion, peeled and sliced

1 bell pepper, seeded and sliced

½ pound fresh mushrooms, sliced

1 loaf soft French bread

4 slices American cheese

Place meat in a covered glass baking dish or heavy-duty zip-close bag. Combine beer and 1½ cups steak sauce; pour over steak. Refrigerate overnight.

Remove steak from marinade and rub generously with your favorite seasoning. Set meat aside to rest while you preheat your grill to 325°.

Grill, covered, for upwards of 45 minutes to an hour (or more depending on the size of your cut and your grill). Only turn meat a few times, rotating to evenly cook. Keep grill cover closed as much as possible.

Combine remaining ½ cup steak sauce with half the melted butter and baste meat with it the last few minutes of cook time. Grill until you have an internal temperature between 135° and 140°. Remove from grill and allow to rest 8 to 10 minute before slicing.

While meat is finishing and resting, grill veggies in a grill basket. Brush bread with remaining melted butter and place on grill, cut side down, until toasted. Move bread to upper rack, top with meat, veggies and cheese; continue to grill until cheese is melted.

Slice into equal servings and serve hot.

Grilled Philly Cheese Steak Sandwiches

Legend has it that Philadelphians Pat and Harry Olivieri are often credited with inventing the sandwich by serving chopped steak and onion on an Italian roll in the early 1930s. You can still visit the original restaurant in Philly, Pat's King of Steaks. When you order, be ready to order "Wit" or "Wit-out" onions. You can even catch Sylvester Stallone standing in line for a sandwich from Pat's King of Steaks in the 1976 movie "Rocky."

1½ pounds boneless beef (top-round or ribeye), cut into thin strips

2 teaspoons seasoning salt

Worcestershire sauce to taste

Black pepper to taste

1 medium green bell pepper, seeded and sliced

1 medium red bell pepper, seeded and sliced

1 medium onion, peeled and sliced

2 tablespoons olive oil

6 soft hoagie-style deli buns

6 to 12 slices provolone cheese

OPTIONAL SAUCE:

⅓ cup mayonnaise

2 to 3 tablespoons Dijon mustard

2 dashes Worcestershire sauce

Season steak with seasoning salt, Worcestershire and pepper. Grill over medium-high heat about 5 minutes or just until cooked through. Be careful to not overcook it.

Once grilled, move to a foil pan and place on a cooler area of the grill. The meat will continue to cook while resting.

Toss veggies and oil in a bowl until evenly coated. Grill at the same time you're grilling the steaks.

Divide meat between buns and top with grilled vegetables. Layer each with a slice or 2 of cheese and wrap in foil. Place on top rack of grill over low heat to allow cheese to melt and bun to steam.

Serve hot with a side of sauce.

For Sauce: Combine all ingredients in a bowl.

If you have leftover steak on hand, that works just as well for this recipe. Just reheat it on the grill for a few minutes.

FOIL PACKET MAGIC

FOIL PACKET COOKING TIPS:

- Take care to not over-stuff your packets. You want enough foil to seal them nicely. To allow even cooking, don't make them too big or vary the sizes too much.

- Double wrap if needed, especially if using light-duty foil.

- Resist turning too often. This will reduce the risk of tearing the foil and juices spilling out.

- Some recipes lend themselves to using foil pans covered with foil. The advantage is that you can open foil to stir and check the progress. This is perfect for feeding a crowd.

- Unless you use nonstick foil, you should always use a bit of nonstick spray on your foil sheets.

Sizzling Starters

Classic Franks and Beans Foil Pack with a Man-Sized Grilling Twist

1 (16-ounce) package hot dogs, 1 inch chopped

1 smoked sausage, 1 inch chopped

1 (28-ounce) can baked beans (not pork and beans)

1 onion, chopped into large pieces

1 green or red bell pepper, chopped into large pieces

½ cup barbecue sauce

2 tablespoons pepper jelly

Combine all ingredients in a bowl. Fill 4 to 6 foil packets with equal portions. Pinch packets closed and grill over medium-high heat about 30 minutes, turning occasionally.

MAN-SIZED TWIST:

There are unlimited ingredients that you can add to the mix. I've tossed in corn, potatoes, assorted vegetables and even store-bought meat balls.

WHO INVENTED ALUMINUM FOIL?

Tin foil was the first lightweight foil to hit the market, but by 1910, it had been replaced by aluminum foil. That's when the first aluminum foil rolling plant was opened in Emmishofen, Switzerland, by J.G. Neher & Sons. Many still refer to aluminum foil as tin foil. In the US, aluminum foil use began around 1913 as a wrap for manufactured candy bars.

Easy Oriental-Style Pork and Pineapple Foil Pack

Start off in a skillet on the stove or the side burner of your grill. Then finish things off on the grill in a foil packet. A great way to season these is with leftover packets of sauce from your last carry-out Chinese meal.

1 tablespoon vegetable oil

1 pound thin-sliced pork chops

3½ tablespoons soy sauce, divided

1 teaspoon oriental five spice seasoning

1 (8-ounce) can pineapple chunks

1 (8-ounce) can sliced water chestnuts

1 green bell pepper, diced

1 onion, sliced

1 (8.5-ounce) can sweet peas, drained

Ginger, allspice, salt and pepper to taste

Heat oil in skillet. Add pork, ½ tablespoon soy sauce and five spice seasoning; brown lightly. (Don't overcook.)

Drain pineapple, reserving juice.

Prepare 8 large squares of foil, 2 for each packet. Place equal portions of pork into center of 4 pieces of foil.

Divide pineapple, water chestnuts, bell pepper, onion and peas between each piece of foil.

In a bowl, combine pineapple juice with ginger, allspice, salt and pepper to taste. Add remaining 3 tablespoons soy sauce.

Fold foil to seal packets. Cook over a medium-hot preheated grill about 5 minutes on each side to steam vegetables. Turn a few times to evenly cook and allow seasoning sauce to distribute evenly in foil. Serve hot.

Beef and Cheddar Potatoes

½ pound ground beef

Salt and pepper to taste

½ cup chopped onion

4 medium potatoes, cubed (skin on or skin off, it's your choice)

1 (4-ounce) can sliced mushrooms

2 tablespoons butter, melted

2 tablespoons real bacon bits

2 to 3 tablespoons water

1½ cups shredded Cheddar cheese

Brown ground beef in a skillet with salt, pepper and onion; drain.

Preheat grill to medium heat. In a foil pan coated with nonstick spray, place potatoes and beef along with remaining ingredients, except cheese. Stir gently to mix. Cover with foil and grill 20 to 30 minutes with grill cover closed.

After 20 minutes, check every 5 minutes; it is done when potatoes are soft but not falling apart.

Before serving, stir in 1 cup cheese and top with remaining ½ cup cheese.

Sizzling Starters

Oktoberfest Sausage, Potato and Cabbage Packets with Mustard Beer Sauce

A great combination of flavors for your Oktoberfest celebration, this recipe is super easy.

1 pound link sausage

1 small head cabbage, cut into large pieces

8 small red potatoes, skin-on and cubed

1 onion, sliced

Salt and pepper to taste

½ teaspoon caraway seed

MUSTARD BEER SAUCE:

1 cup Dijon mustard

¼ to ½ cup beer

2 tablespoons sour cream

1 tablespoon brown sugar

2 teaspoons hot sauce

Salt and pepper to taste

Heat grill to medium high and prepare 4 to 6 large heavy-duty foil sheets. Prep foil with nonstick spray. If desired, grill sausage about 2 minutes on each side before slicing. Cut sausage into 1-inch pieces.

Place sausage, cabbage, potatoes and onion in a large bowl. Add salt, pepper and caraway seed; mix everything to coat evenly.

Divide mixture evenly between foil packets then seal each one. Grill about 35 minutes, turning as needed. Serve hot topped with Mustard Beer Sauce.

For Sauce: Combine mustard and ¼ cup beer in a bowl. Add remaining ingredients and taste. Add a dash or 2 of water to thin slightly, if needed. Add additional beer if you like a heartier hops flavor.

PIZZA ON THE GRILL

GRILLED PIZZA TIPS:

- Charcoal, wood, and even a gas grill will work fine.
- Your grill needs to have a cover; keep it closed as much as possible when grilling pizza.
- Wood chips add the flavor of wood-fired pizza ovens. Consider wood chips from fruit trees, as well as the standard grilling woods such as hickory.

CRUST TIPS:

The trick to cooking a crust on the grill is to not burn the bottom before the toppings are done. Keep temps low and take advantage of upper racks.

- PREBAKED CRUSTS are perfect for most recipes and can be found in a variety of sizes.
- UNCOOKED AND CANNED DOUGH: If you choose to use dough then I suggest using a grilling pizza tray. Make your crusts smaller so they will be easier to work with.
- ASSORTED BREADS AS A CRUST: You can use anything from Texas toast to French bread loaves, English muffins, and more. My favorite is puffy flatbread from the deli section.

GRILL TALK: Use any type of precooked meats that you would use on homemade pizza — pepperoni, browned and crumbled beef or sausage, grilled and chopped or pulled chicken, etc.

Sizzling Starters

Quick and Easy Grilled Garlic French Bread Chicken Parmesan Pizza

Next time you're at the store grab one of those huge French bread loaves from the deli that's covered with butter and garlic. Then, follow the steps below for a crazy good version of a French bread pizza.

1 large loaf garlic French bread

½ cup white Alfredo sauce or traditional pizza sauce

Grilled chicken, cubed or chopped

Sliced black olives

Italian seasoning

Red pepper flakes

Mozzarella cheese

Parmesan cheese

Anything else you want to add!

Top the sliced French Garlic bread with sauce, grilled chicken and olives. Add seasonings as desired. Top with cheese. (Remember, the French bread is already cooked, as is the chicken. All you're really doing is grilling long enough to heat the added toppings and melt the cheese.)

Grill over medium heat on a top rack if possible with the grill lid closed. If you grill over too high of heat you may make the bread crust too crunchy or burn it.

Grill until the cheese is melted and bubbly; allow to rest for a few minutes before slicing and serving.

Kent's Hickory-Smoked Grilled Barbecue Pizza

Let's start this selection of pizza recipes with one of my favorite versions – a grilled pizza with hickory-smoked pulled pork. What's perfect about this recipe is that you can make it with simple ingredients and leftovers.

WHAT YOU'LL NEED:

1 to 2 pizza crusts: I use prepared pizza crusts that I find at my local grocery store near the pizza and spaghetti making supplies. The brand I buy comes packaged with 2 crusts, completely cooked, and ready to go.

Barbecue sauce for your pizza sauce: Depending on how much sauce you like will determine how much to use. For 2 pizzas I generally use just over a cup of my favorite store-bought sauce or my homemade sauce.

Meat: First you'll 1 to 2 cups hickory-smoked pulled pork barbecue, preferably the kind not coated in sauce already. But if that's all you have, then that's okay. You can use your own hickory-smoked pulled pork or pick some up from your favorite barbecue joint.

Cheese: Pick any cheese you like that melts well.

Other Toppings: At this point you can add whatever you want. I like my Hickory Smoked Grilled Barbecue Pizzas to be pretty simple to maintain the barbecue flavors that I enjoy, but feel free to toss on some pizza topping items that you enjoy.

TO ASSEMBLE:

Place pizza crusts on a covered grill; preheat to medium-low heat. Top each with barbecue sauce. (Don't add too much, just enough for flavor.) Top each with about a quarter of the pork, then some of the cheese; repeat. (Add additional toppings, if desired). Grill about 10 minutes, or until the cheese is melted and the toppings and crust are heated through. Serve hot!

Grilled Pita Bread Goat Cheese Spinach Pizzas

4 whole pita breads, not halved or broken open

Olive oil

Grated Parmesan cheese

Garlic salt

Pizza sauce

Tomato, thinly cut slices or large chopped

Red onion slices

Spinach leaves, blanched or thawed and drained frozen

Black olives

1 package goat cheese, crumbled

Italian seasoning

Brush a small amount of olive oil on each piece of pita bread and sprinkle with grated Parmesan cheese and garlic salt.

You can grill the pita bread slightly if you are allowing people to build their own pizzas. If you do pre-grill the crusts, be sure to use the upper rack as you don't want to burn the pita bread.

Add sauce, toppings, cheese, and dashes of Italian seasoning to your pizza.

Grill on a covered grill over medium-high heat. Use an upper rack if needed; close lid; grill until cheese is melted, bubbled, with golden edges.

Sizzling Starters

Grilled Cast-Iron Deep-Dish Pizza

Grab your trusted cast-iron skillet and get ready for some deep-dish pizza right off the grill.

- 2 tablespoons oil
- 1 pizza crust
- ¼ to ½ cup pizza sauce
- ½ cup diced pepperoni or ham
- Your favorite toppings: onion, bell pepper, black olives, etc.
- ½ cup shredded mozzarella cheese
- ½ cup grated Parmesan cheese

Preheat a covered grill to medium high. Place oil in iron skillet and place on grill to preheat.

Prepare dough and allow it to rise slightly. (If you are using store-bought crust, follow package directions.) Place the crust in prepared cast-iron skillet, pressing dough up sides about ½ inch, being careful since the skillet is hot.

Spread pizza sauce over flat part of crust. Top with meat and your favorite toppings. Cover with cheese.

Grilling time will vary due to your grill, heat, thickness of crust and how many toppings you pile on. Cooking time could be from about 30 minutes to almost an hour.

Allow the pizza to rest for a few minutes before slicing and serving.

GRILL TALK:
Take care not to burn your crust. The cast iron will remain hot for a quite a while. So start off over the heat, move to a spot... then to an upper rack to finish things off.

DOGS, BRATS & OTHER LINKS

HOT DIGGITY DOG! Links on a bun are a favorite for tailgating because they are so easy to cook and eat. Links come in all sorts of varieties. There's the all-American hot dog, of course, but there are many other delicious alternatives to put on your bun with roots from around the world — bratwurst, chorizo, kielbasa, knackwurst, bangers, andouille and smoked sausage — but we'll concentrate on just a few in this section.

Hot dogs are as American as, well, hot dogs! Many states and major cities in the good ol' USA seem to have their own unique version. But your typical hot dog started out grilled, topped with a few condiments (mustard, pickle relish and chopped onion) and served up on a plain hot dog bun. It became the favorite food at America's favorite pastime — you guessed it — baseball games! Local vendors at ball parks across the country have taken to specializing the dogs, condiments and other menu items to their geographic area and local customers' tastes, and some baseball parks even have signature dogs, like the Boston Fenway Frank.

Who is Frank, you say? Frank is just one of the many nicknames for a hot dog that have popped up over the years — frankfurter, wiener, weenie, redhot, and even bow-wow.

Hot dogs can be boiled, baked, grilled or steamed. I know that several regional hot dogs are never grilled and hot dog purists would only boil or steam them. I say grilling just makes them better, but I really just want everyone to enjoy their favorite dogs prepared how they like them best. Then grab some peanuts, a cold beverage, and yell "PLAY BALL!"

Sizzling Starters

Boston Fenway Frank

Settle in and watch a Red Sox game while munching down on a Fenway Frank. Even a Braves fan like me can appreciate this simple concoction – especially the bun.

Tailgate Friendly

All beef hot dogs

Fresh New England-style hot dog buns

Yellow mustard

Pickle relish

Boil hot dogs on the stove or using your grill's side burner then grill just long enough to get grill marks. Place bun on grill to get warm but not toasted.

Place hot dog in bun and top with a general helping of yellow mustard and a nice scoop of pickle relish.

New England-style hot dog buns are split on the top, not on the side like regular hot dog buns. If you can't find them in your local grocery, a regular bun will do!

Martinsville Racing Hot Dog

If you're a NASCAR fan and have visited the track at Martinsville, Virginia, you probably already know two things. The really cool trophy they give to race winners are handmade grandfather clocks, and the famous Martinsville Speedway hot dog is super delicious. The original dogs were from the Jesse Jones Company and were served at the track for more than 60 years. My version still uses the traditional Jesse Jones hot dog.

Jesse Jones Southern-Style hot dogs

Hot dog buns, warmed

Yellow mustard

Chili

I keep my Jesse Jones Southern-Style hot dogs in a water and beer bath on the grill until needed.

Then I slap them on the hot grates to add a few grill marks before putting them in a lightly steamed or toasted bun with a splash of yellow mustard and a scoop of hot chili.

THE MARTINSVILLE CLOCK

- The first grandfather clock given as a Martinsville trophy was in 1964 and was made a few miles from the track at Ridgeway Clocks.

- Freddy Lorenzen won the first clock.

- In 2004, the Ridgeway Clock Company was bought by the Howard Miller Co. and production was moved to Zeeland, Michigan.

- Richard Petty has twelve Martinsville Speedway Clocks, more than any other driver. .

Sizzling Starters

Coney Island

Local lore says that back in the day, immigrants were confused by the American term "hot dog," thinking the meat was actually made of dogs. The solution was an early 1900's law around the Coney Island area that prohibited the use of the term "hot dog" in favor of ordering a "Coney Island."

Beef or pork hot dogs

Fresh buns

Coney Meat Sauce

Yellow mustard

Finely chopped onions

CONEY MEAT SAUCE:

1 pound ground beef

1 onion, finely chopped

⅓ cup water

2 tablespoons ketchup

1 tablespoon yellow mustard

1½ tablespoons apple cider vinegar

½ tablespoon Worcestershire sauce

Dash sugar

Coney Island hot dogs are most often steamed. You can steam hot dogs on the grill simply by grilling them slowly over medium heat while wrapped in foil with a spoonful or two of water.

Warm bun slightly on grill before putting dog in bun.

Top with Coney Meat Sauce, a line of yellow mustard and chopped onions to taste.

For Sauce: Brown meat with onion, breaking up the meat to a fine texture while it cooks; drain.

Add remaining ingredients and cook until reduced and almost dried out, 35 to 40 minutes.

Grilled Corn Chip and Chopped Chili Dog

I love using plumper hot dogs with this recipe. If you don't want to make chili from scratch, grab some at a nearby store or restaurant.

Hot dogs

Buns

Corn chips

Kent's Beer Chili

Cheese

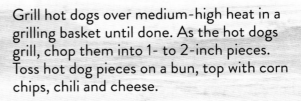

KENT'S BEER CHILI:

½ pound ground beef

½ pound ground sausage

1 tablespoon minced garlic

1 (8-ounce) can tomato sauce

2 (15-ounce) cans chili beans

1 (1.25-ounce) envelope hot chili seasoning

2 teaspoons cumin powder

2 teaspoons cayenne pepper

1 tablespoon minced jalapeño

1 (14-ounce) can diced tomatoes

½ (12-ounce) can beer

1 small onion, chopped

Hot sauce to taste

Cornmeal to thicken

Grill hot dogs over medium-high heat in a grilling basket until done. As the hot dogs grill, chop them into 1- to 2-inch pieces. Toss hot dog pieces on a bun, top with corn chips, chili and cheese.

For Chili: Cook ground beef and sausage with garlic in frying pan until cooked through; drain. Combine with remaining ingredients in a large pot.

Simmer 2 hours over medium heat, covered, adding additional water or beer as needed.

Sizzling Starters

Cincinnati Chili Cheese Dog

Tailgate Friendly

Cincinnati is known for hot dogs featuring chili and cheese. So, what makes this hot dog different from a regular chili dog? Cincinnati style chili is sweeter with a hint of chocolate and cinnamon. Cincinnati dogs are generally steamed or boiled but the grilled version is a hit at tailgates. If grilling is ok with Cincinnati football fans, then it's good enough for me.

Grilled hot dogs

Fresh buns

Cincinnati-Style Chili

Shredded Cheddar cheese

Diced onions

CINCINNATI-STYLE CHILI:

1 pound ground beef

½ cup water

1 onion, finely chopped

1 (8-ounce) can tomato sauce

1 tablespoon vinegar

2 teaspoons Worcestershire sauce

2 to 3 teaspoons minced garlic

1 ounce unsweetened chocolate

¼ cup chili powder

1 teaspoon salt

1 teaspoon ground cumin

1 teaspoon ground cinnamon

½ teaspoon ground cayenne pepper

Dash allspice

2 to 3 cloves, optional

Put grilled hot dog in bun and top with chili, cheese and onion.

For Chili: Brown ground beef; drain well. Add water and onion; cook until onions are soft.

Add remaining ingredients. Simmer 2 to 3 hours, adding just enough water as needed to keep the chili from burning. (You don't want a drippy chili for this recipe.)

Dogs, Brats & Other Links

Chicago-Style Hot Dogs

This is one of my wife Ally's favorite hot dogs. She loves the poppy seed bun and that the dog has been "drug through the garden."

Kosher-style all-beef hot dogs, grilled

Poppy seed hot dog buns, steamed or warmed

Yellow mustard

Sweet pickle relish

Chopped white onion

Fresh tomato wedges

Dill pickle spears

Pepperoncini peppers

Dash celery salt

Place grilled hot dogs on warm poppy seed buns. Add toppings and sprinkle with a dash of celery salt.

Don't add ketchup or you're kicked out of the Chicago-Style Hot Dog Club.

TO DRAG YOUR DOG THROUGH THE GARDEN: Add any or all of the following: cucumber slices, bite-sized sport peppers, green bell pepper slices, and even some shredded lettuce!

Kansas City Kraut Dog

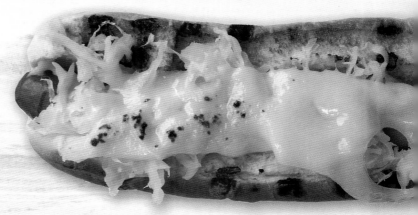

Grilled pork or beef hot dogs

Lightly toasted sesame seed buns

Warmed sauerkraut

Brown mustard

White American cheese or Swiss cheese slices

Place grilled hot dog on a toasted sesame seed bun topped with warmed sauerkraut. Add a generous amount of brown mustard. Place cheese on top and melt slightly.

West Virginia Slaw (or No Slaw) Dog

One of my favorite states for grabbing a hot dog is West Virginia. Some West Virginians swear that slaw is a required topping while others say that only chili is best. I see a Hatfield-and-McCoy-style feud breaking out.

Really plump hot dogs

Fresh soft hot dog buns

Chili

Yellow or spicy mustard

Sweet coleslaw or Kent's Creamy Buttermilk Coleslaw (page 254)

Grill hot dogs and place each on a bun. Top with a hearty serving of chili and a big squirt of mustard. Finish with a big spoonful of coleslaw to top things off.

Marinated Hot Sauce Beef Dogs

Tailgate Friendly

I suggest using this recipe with generic all-beef hot dogs. To get the flavor of this marinade past the outer barrier or casing of the hot dog, cut them lightly on two or more sides to a depth of about ⅛ inch or poke a bunch of holes in each dog.

1 package all-beef bun-size hot dogs

½ (12-ounce) can beer

1 (3-ounce) bottle hot sauce

¼ cup steak sauce

Hot dog buns, bread or pita wrap

Gently cut each hot dog lengthwise in three places from tip to top to a ⅛-inch depth. (Or use a fork to poke several holes along the dogs. Don't do too many or the hot dog may fall apart when cooking.)

Combine beer, hot sauce and steak sauce in a zip-close bag. Add hot dogs and marinate in the refrigerator several hours (overnight if possible).

Grill dogs over medium-high heat until grill marks appear. Transfer to a foil pan, coat with remaining marinade and continue to grill another 10 to 15 minutes.

Serve hot on your favorite bun.

Mickey Mouse's first on screen words were "Hot Dog!" marking his transition from the silent screen to talking pictures.

Tennessee-Style Smoked Sausage Dog

I live in Tennessee and heard a ton of debate about what constitutes a Tennessee-style hot dog. The suggestions ranged from a hot dog on a bun with mustard only to variations that included Jack Daniels barbecue sauce and pulled pork. Hey, I like that. Fans of the University of Tennessee football team overwhelmingly preferred a smoked sausage in place of a hot dog. So, in honor of all of my family and friends who are Volunteer football fans, I'm suggesting a Tennessee-Style Smoked Sausage...Dog.

Smoked sausage

Barbecue sauce (yes, Jack Daniels style is fine)

Hot dog buns

Pulled hickory-smoked barbecue

Sweet onions, thinly sliced

Coleslaw

Cut smoked sausage into bun-sized sections; baste with barbecue sauce and grill until hot. Place sausage on a bun and top with barbecue meat, barbecue sauce, onions and slaw.

Southwestern Green Chile Grilled Franks with Grilled Lemon Lime Avocado Slices

Tailgate Friendly

This recipe is as big as Texas when it comes to flavor but as simple as counting to three.

10 to 12 all-beef hot dogs

1 (15-ounce) jar salsa

1 (4-ounce) can green chiles, drained

Dash chili powder

Dash cumin powder

Texas toast

Chopped onions

Grilled Avocados

Grill hot dogs over medium high-heat. While hot dogs grill, heat salsa in a small saucepan or in microwave.

Place green chiles in a small saucepan (or microwave-safe bowl) and top with chili powder and cumin; heat.

Butter Texas toast and grill until lightly toasted.

Place hot dogs on Texas Toast and top with salsa, chiles, onion and Grilled Avocados.

GRILLED AVOCADOS:

2 avocados, seeded and sliced

Olive oil

1 lemon, juiced

1 lime, juiced

Salt and pepper to taste

For Avocados: Baste avocado slices lightly in olive oil. Grill avocado slices over medium-high heat while drizzling with lemon and lime juice. Grill just enough to add grill marks, about 2 minutes per side. (Do not overcook as avocados will become too soft.)

Sprinkle with salt and pepper to taste before removing from grill.

Sizzling Starters

Classic Beer Bratwursts with Grilled Sauerkraut

8 to 12 bratwursts

1 (12-ounce) can beer

½ onion, sliced

½ bell pepper, sliced

1 (15-ounce) can sauerkraut, drained

Dash salt and pepper

Preheat grill to medium high. Combine bratwursts, beer, onion and bell pepper in a heavy-duty foil pan on the grill.

Every 3 minutes, remove brats from marinade and cook on grill 3 minutes, then return to marinade 3 minutes. Repeat this process for a total of 15 minutes.

While bratwursts cook, heat sauerkraut in a foil pan prepped with nonstick spray.

Remove cooked brats from marinade and place on hot grill for a few moments to crisp the outer skin.

Drain veggies, discarding marinade. Place a bratwurst on a bun topped with veggies and steaming hot sauerkraut. Season with salt and pepper.

Apple Cider Brown Sugar Bratwursts

Apples and pork just seem to go together. So, it stands to reason that apple cider and pork bratwurst would go together.

6 bratwursts

1 cup apple cider or apple juice

½ onion, sliced

½ tablespoon brown sugar

Preheat grill to medium-low heat. In a large heavy-duty foil pan, combine bratwursts, apple cider, onion and brown sugar. Place pan on grill to simmer.

Rotate bratwursts between grill grates and apple cider bath, grilling bratwursts for a few minutes then returning to bath to baste.

Before placing on a bun, make sure to grill the bratwursts for a final minute or two.

Sizzling Starters

Spicy Beer Brats with Quick Pepper Jack Beer Sauce

Tailgate Friendly

Add a little spice to your bratwursts with this fun recipe.

6 bratwursts

½ (12-ounce) can beer

Jalapeño slices to taste

6 buns or hoagie rolls, toasted

1 onion, sliced

½ bell pepper, sliced

Pepper Jack Beer Sauce

PEPPER JACK BEER SAUCE:

½ (12-ounce) can beer

4 ounces cream cheese

½ pound pepper jack cheese

Preheat grill to medium high. Place brats in a foil pan on the grill; add beer and jalapeño slices. Simmer 10 to 15 minutes.

Remove brats from beer bath and place over high heat to brown the outside. Serve hot on a toasted bun with onion, bell pepper and Pepper Jack Beer Sauce.

For Sauce: Combine all ingredients in a saucepan over medium heat. As cheese melts, increase heat slightly and cook about 5 minutes.

Reduce heat to low and cook, stirring constantly, until sauce reaches your desired consistency. Serve hot.

This Pepper Jack Beer Sauce is also delicious served over a burger — or double the recipe and serve with chips for dipping.

Andouille Sausage & Shrimp Po'Boys

4 to 6 andouille sausage links

24 medium shrimp, shelled and deveined

Olive oil

Seafood seasoning to taste

1 bell pepper, thinly sliced

Creole seasoning to taste

Butter

4 to 6 French bread rolls (or Italian-style hoagie buns)

2 tomatoes, sliced

½ onion, thinly sliced

½ head lettuce, shredded

Grill andouille sausage over medium-high heat.

Place shrimp in a grill pan, baste with oil and sprinkle with seafood seasoning. Add bell pepper and cook until shrimp are cooked through.

As sausage browns, add to grill pan and mix all together, seasoning to taste with Cajun seasoning.

Lightly butter rolls and heat on grill.

Serve sausage and shrimp hot off the grill with bell peppers on toasted rolls. Top with tomatoes, onion and lettuce. Top with Cheater's Rèmoulade Sauce and serve immediately.

CHEATER'S RÈMOULADE SAUCE:

⅓ cup Thousand Island dressing

¼ cup mayonnaise

2 tablespoons Dijon mustard

1½ tablespoons relish

2 teaspoons chili powder

Combine ingredients in a bowl and mix well.

Sizzling Starters

Chorizo Sausage with Corn Salsa

6 to 8 chorizo sausages in casing

1 (12-ounce) bottle Mexican beer

1 lime, juiced

6 to 8 buns or flour tortillas

Chipotle Corn Salsa

6 to 8 white American or pepper jack cheese slices

Shredded iceberg lettuce and sour cream, optional

CHIPOTLE CORN SALSA:

1 (15-ounce) can whole-kernel corn, drained

1 tomato, chopped

1 jalapeño, seeded and chopped

½ tablespoon minced garlic

½ tablespoon ground chipotle powder

1 tablespoon olive oil

½ tablespoon apple cider vinegar

2 teaspoons lime juice

2 teaspoons cumin powder

Dash cilantro

Dash salt and pepper

⅛ teaspoon ground cumin

Combine sausage, beer and lime juice in a foil pan; place on grill over medium-high heat. Cook about 10 minutes or until sausages are hot.

Remove sausage to grill grates to add grill marks and to complete cooking. Baste with some of the liquid in the foil pan as you turn.

Serve hot on a bun or warmed flour tortilla with Chipotle Corn Salsa, cheese and your choice of additional toppings, such as shredded lettuce and sour cream.

For Salsa: Combine all ingredients in a bowl and mix well. Cover and chill before serving.

Serious
GRILLING

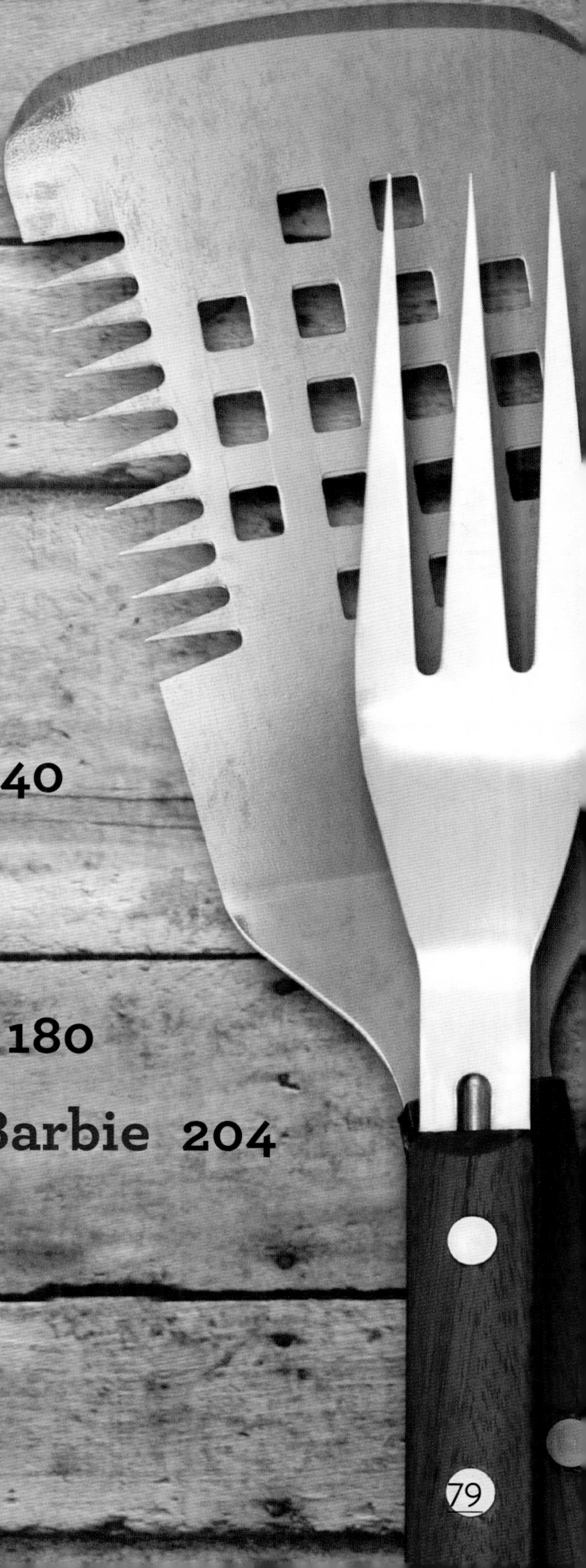

BIG TIME BURGERS

BEEF IS TOPS FOR BURGERS.

Choose beef with a mix of 80/20 – that's 80% beef and 20% fat. A fat content ratio less than 20% may make for a leaner burger but it will also lack flavor. A higher fat content may cause flare ups on the grill and the burgers will shrink more as the fat burns off.

A burger patty should be about six ounces — that's a little larger than a baseball. Form a ball then flatten it out until it's about three-fourths of an inch thick and circular in shape.

Why do some people put a dent in the middle of a burger before cooking? Ground beef tends to contract as it cooks. The outside heats up faster than the inside so the burger shrinks from the edges and puffs up. Putting a small dent in the patty before cooking helps the burger to keep a flatter shape as it cooks.

SOME TIPS FOR GRILLING THE BEST BEEF BURGERS:

1) Grill your burgers over high heat to sear the outside.
2) Avoid using your spatula to press down on your burgers while cooking.
3) Flip your burgers only one time – cook about three minutes on each side for medium rare plus.
4) If you get a flare up, cover the grill.
5) Allow your burgers to rest for a few minutes before serving.

Not every burger has to be made with beef and covered with plain old ketchup! So I have included recipes using a variety of meats and ingredients that make for a lighter meal that will also light up your taste buds with flavor.

Serious Grilling

Kent's Basic Beef Burger

Allow me to start this section with a Basic Ground Beef Burger with minimal seasoning. Think of this as a starting point for a whole bunch of great tasting burgers.

1½ pounds ground beef or sirloin (80/20 fat ratio)

Salt and pepper to taste

4 to 6 hamburger buns

Condiments (mayonnaise, ketchup, mustard, etc.)

Toppings (lettuce, onion, tomato, etc.)

Slices of your favorite cheese, optional

Make 4 to 6 patties, being careful not to overwork the meat. Sprinkle with salt and pepper on both sides. Grill to an internal temp of 160°. Prep your bun with your favorite condiments and toppings and serve up your hot and juicy hamburger.

For Cheeseburger: Before removing the burgers from the grill, pat any excess grease off the top of burgers with a paper towel. Use a pair of tongs so you don't burn yourself. Reduce heat, add your cheese and allow a few moments for melting.

FIVE BURGER TOPPING OPTIONS FOR SPRUCING UP A BORING BURGER!

Start with my basic burger recipe then make it special with these suggestions – in case you want to change things up a bit.

Driving Miss Cheesy: It's a tasty burger alternative inspired by southern life. Top your grilled burger with fresh pimento cheese, a slice of southern-style fried green tomato and maybe some chow chow. Just in case you don't know what chow chow is...it's a crunchy and zesty relish-like condiment made with chopped cabbage. All of these ingredients combine for a flavor-packed burger.

Pulled Pork Barbecue Burger: Why not top your grilled ground beef or ground pork burger with slow hickory-smoked, hand-pulled pork barbecue? The flavor combination is amazing. If you don't have a smoker, or time to slow smoke a Boston butt, pick up some pork barbecue at your local joint (that's barbecue talk for BBQ restaurant). While you're at it, toss on some coleslaw.

Surf and Turf Burger: Yep, a burger topped with grilled shrimp, crisp lettuce and a dash of seafood seasoning. For a little more flavor, add some orange juice to your favorite barbecue sauce and brush it over the shrimp. Yum.

Duck Meat Burger: If you love wild game, this burger is for you. Cook a ground venison burger then top it with grilled or smoked, pulled duck breast. Top it off with a slice of your favorite cheese and a spoonful of barbecue sauce.

Kent's Stuffed Cheeseburgers

This is one of my favorite hamburger recipes because it's so versatile. My recipe calls for cheese as a stuffing, but you can also use onions, mushrooms, jalapeños or a combination of all of the above.

1½ pounds ground beef

1 tablespoon butter, softened

2 teaspoons garlic powder

2 tablespoons steak sauce

4 cheese slices

Combine meat, butter, garlic powder and steak sauce. To make 4 burgers, you'll need 8 patties, so divide meat into 8 equal amounts and form into very thin patties.

For each burger, place a slice of cheese onto 1 patty, making sure it does not overreach the edge. (Break off extra cheese and place in middle.) Place another patty over cheese and press edges together. Chill to set as you prep your grill.

Grill until cooked through. Serve on your favorite bun with your favorite toppings.

STUFFED BURGER TIPS: Don't overstuff the burgers because the meat contracts as it cooks and an overstuffed burger may break apart on the grill. Also, don't overcook these burgers or the cheese will tend to ooze out.

The foil cooking method works great for these burgers. Place each patty on a square of nonstick foil (or foil treated with nonstick spray) and cook until patty firms up enough to turn. When you flip the patty, gently peel the foil off.

Serious Grilling

Shredded Cheeseburgers with Zesty Steak Sauce Ketchup

1½ pounds ground beef

1 cup shredded cheese

Salt and pepper to taste

Soft yeast rolls

ZESTY STEAK SAUCE KETCHUP:

½ cup ketchup

½ cup steak sauce

½ tablespoon melted butter

2 tablespoons water

Combine beef, cheese, salt and pepper; form into 4 to 6 patties. Cook on grill and serve with Zesty Steak Sauce Ketchup on yeast rolls.

For Sauce: Place all ingredients in a saucepan and simmer about 10 minutes or until well combined. Best served warm.

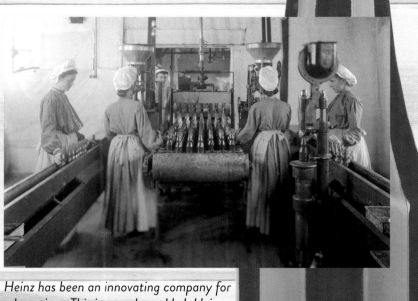

Heinz has been an innovating company for a long time. This image shows H. J. Heinz Company Ketchup Bottling Department as it appeared in 1904. Note the assembly line conveyor belt, sanitary hair nets, aprons, and matching uniforms.

H. J. Heinz Company Photographs, MSP 57, Detre Library & Archives, Heinz History Center, Pittsburgh, Pa.

Tidwell's Tailgate Pimento Cheeseburger

Our friend Jerry Tidwell shares this Pimento Cheeseburger
that is a staple at South Carolina tailgate parties and backyard cookouts.
Jerry is a University of Tennessee fan, but gives credit to his sons who
went to South Carolina and turned Jerry into a fan of one of the famous
hamburgers in the South Eastern Conference.

2 pounds ground chuck

1 tablespoon minced garlic

2 tablespoons minced onion

3 tablespoons steak sauce

1 to 2 tablespoons yellow
   mustard

Salt and pepper to taste

Buns

Pimento Cheese

PIMENTO CHEESE:

1 (3-ounce) jar chopped
   pimentos, drained

3 ounces cream cheese,
   softened

1½ cups coarsely grated sharp
   Cheddar cheese

1½ cups coarsely grated pepper
   jack cheese

3 tablespoons mayonnaise

Combine ground chuck, garlic, onion, steak
sauce, mustard, salt and pepper; form into 6
to 8 patties. (Or 12 small patties for sliders.)
Grill over medium-high heat. Serve on a
bun topped with Pimento Cheese.

For Pimento Cheese: Mix all ingredients
together in a bowl, cover and chill before
serving.

For tailgating, you can form the Pimento
Cheese into burger-sized patties, place
them on wax paper and chill or freeze
before heading to the game.

Serious Grilling

Big Ole' Bacon Pub Burger

4 slices bacon

1½ pounds 80/20 ground beef

1½ tablespoons Monterey Steak Seasoning

3 tablespoons butter

1 sweet onion, sliced

Steak sauce

4 slices Cheddar cheese

4 lettuce leaves

4 tomato slices

4 buns, toasted

MONTEREY STEAK SEASONING:

2 tablespoons sea salt

1 tablespoon coarse-ground black pepper

1 tablespoon dried onion powder

2½ teaspoons garlic powder

2 teaspoons crushed red pepper flakes

1½ teaspoons thyme

1½ teaspoons rosemary

1½ teaspoons fennel seed, optional

Cook bacon crispy and drain on paper towels; set aside. Mix ground beef and steak seasoning; form into 4 to 6 patties. Place on grill and cook to desired temperature.

While burgers cook, make a foil packet for butter and onion; place in hottest spot of grill to cook until burgers are ready.

Before you remove burgers from grill, baste generously with steak sauce and cover with cheese. When cheese is melted, serve burgers topped with bacon, grilled onions, lettuce and tomato on a toasted bun.

For Seasoning: Combine all, mixing well. Delicious on burgers, steaks and more.

Jumbo Jalapeño Pub Burgers with Green Chile Sauce

1 pound ground beef

1 pound ground pork

2 tablespoons hot sauce

2 tablespoons chopped jalapeños

6 white American cheese slices (or pepper jack cheese slices)

6 buns, toasted

GREEN CHILE SAUCE:

1 (4-ounce) can green chiles

2 teaspoons Cajun seasoning (or chili seasoning)

1 cup sour cream

Combine all ingredients, except cheese. Form into 6 large burgers and grill.

Before removing from grill, top burgers with cheese slices.

Serve hot on a toasted bun with your choice of toppings and Green Chile Sauce.

For Sauce: Mix all together and chill at least 30 minutes before using.

WHAT IS A PUB BURGER?

The term "Pub Burger" seems to have come to describe any fresh burger that's not made on a production line. Another qualifying factor is that it can't be served on a generic bun. Big, juicy, artisan bun, and cool toppings are the requirements for a good "pub burger."

Texas Toast Jalapeño Burgers with Creamy Salsa

I prefer this made with jarred jalapeños rather than fresh. The recipes works with either, but not sweetened jalapeño relish.

1 pound ground sirloin

¼ cup minced jalapeño

1½ tablespoons sour cream

½ tablespoon cumin powder

2 teaspoons chili powder

Dash garlic powder

Salt and pepper to taste

4 tablespoons butter, softened

Texas toast

CREAMY SALSA:

¾ cup prepared salsa

⅓ cup sour cream

1 tablespoon mayonnaise

Dash hot sauce

Dash garlic salt

Dash lemon juice

Mix meat, jalapeño, sour cream and seasonings in a bowl; form into 4 to 6 equal-sized patties. Grill over medium-high heat until done.

Spread butter over Texas toast and grill (or broil in oven) until golden brown and toasted. Build burgers on Texas toast topped with Creamy Salsa and your favorite toppings.

For Salsa: Combine salsa, sour cream and mayonnaise in a bowl. Season to taste with hot sauce, garlic salt and lemon juice.

Serious Grilling

Craft Beer Burgers
with Beer Mustard Sauce

For diversity, choose different beers for the burger and the sauce. A fruit-infused ale works great for the mustard sauce.

1½ pounds ground beef

¼ cup finely chopped onion

½ cup craft beer

2 tablespoons Worcestershire sauce

½ tablespoon minced garlic

1½ teaspoons salt

1 teaspoon pepper

2 cloves garlic, finely chopped

¼ cup breadcrumbs

Pretzel bun, toasted

Pickles

BEER MUSTARD SAUCE:

⅔ cup Dijon mustard

⅓ cup honey

1 cup craft beer

2 tablespoons cornstarch

2 teaspoons red pepper flakes

2 teaspoons minced garlic

¼ cup lemon juice

Combine all ingredients, except bun. Form 4 to 6 patties and grill to your desired temperature.

Serve on a toasted pretzel bun topped with pickles and Beer Mustard Sauce.

For Sauce: Combine everything and chill overnight.

SOMETHING'S BREWING IN THE WHITE HOUSE

President Barack Obama, a craft beer enthusiast, made history when he became the first President to authorize the brewing of craft beer on the White House Grounds. It all started with Mr. Obama purchasing a home brewing kit - with his personal funds. Soon he and the White House Chefs were coming up with ideas for brews. One included honey collected from bee hives on the south lawn.

Source: The White House

Pineapple Stuffed Sweet and Spicy Hamburgers

1½ pounds ground beef

¼ cup soy sauce

2 teaspoons paprika

2 teaspoons chili powder

2 teaspoons minced garlic

1 teaspoon seasoning salt

1 teaspoon ground cumin

1 (8-ounce) can pineapple slices, drained, juice reserved

4 hamburger buns

2 tablespoons Pineapple Ketchup

PINEAPPLE KETCHUP:

Reserved pineapple juice

1 cup ketchup

⅓ cup mustard

½ tablespoon brown sugar or teriyaki sauce

½ tablespoon hot sauce

Dash salt

Mix meat with seasonings. Divide ground beef into 8 equal portions and press each into a thin patty.

Form 2 patties around each pineapple slice so none of the pineapple is showing.

Working gently, place burgers on grill, and cook to well done, turning as few times as possible.

Serve hot on a bun topped with Pineapple Ketchup and your favorite toppings.

For Ketchup: Combine all ketchup ingredients in a saucepan and bring to a boil. Quickly remove from heat, mixing well.

Cool about 5 minutes before serving with burgers.

I love pineapple – they are perfect for any summer grilling get-together. I couldn't decide which of these three recipes for pineapple burgers to include – so I included them all!

Pineapple Teriyaki Hamburgers

This recipe is crazy simple. Grill Kent's Basic Beef Burger (page 81), basting it with teriyaki sauce. While it cooks, grill canned pineapple slices. Serve burgers topped with grilled pineapple on toasted Hawaiian rolls.

Crushed Pineapple and Canadian Bacon Burgers

The sweetness of the pineapple pares perfectly with the salty Canadian bacon.

1 (8-ounce) can crushed pineapple, juice reserved

1 pound ground beef

1 tablespoon teriyaki sauce

1 teaspoon ginger

2 teaspoons garlic powder

Salt and pepper to taste

4 slices Canadian bacon

4 slices mozzarella or Swiss cheese

4 Hawaiian buns, toasted

Drain pineapple, reserving juice in a separate bowl.

Combine beef, teriyaki sauce, ginger, garlic powder and drained pineapple; season to taste with salt and pepper. Form into 4 patties and grill, basting with reserved pineapple juice.

When hamburgers are almost done, toss Canadian bacon slices on grill to heat them up. Top finished burgers with heated bacon and cheese. Serve hot on toasted Hawaiian buns.

Asiago Pressato Cheeseburgers with Caramelized Red Onions

1½ pounds ground beef

1 teaspoon salt

1 teaspoon black pepper

1 tablespoon Dijon mustard

½ teaspoon dried basil, optional

4 to 6 slices Asiago Pressato cheese

4 to 6 hard-crust buns or sliced French bread

Caramelized Red Onions

Romaine lettuce

4 to 6 tomato slices

Garlic-flavored mayonnaise and/or other condiments

CARAMELIZED RED ONIONS:

1 tablespoon olive oil

2 small red onions, thinly sliced

2 teaspoons sugar

¼ teaspoon salt

⅛ teaspoon black pepper

1 tablespoon balsamic vinegar

Combine ground beef with salt, pepper, mustard and basil. Form into 4 to 6 patties. Grill burgers to desired temperature. When removing from grill, immediately top with a slice of cheese.

Serve on a bun with Caramelized Red Onions, romaine lettuce and fresh tomato slices topped with your favorite condiments. It's great with garlic-flavored mayonnaise.

For Onions: Heat oil in a 10-inch nonstick skillet over medium heat. Add onions, sugar, salt and pepper. Reduce heat to medium and cook, stirring occasionally, until golden brown, about 15 minutes. Stir in the vinegar and cook 1 minute longer; remove from heat.

Classic Ranch Burgers on Toasted Sesame Seed Buns

1½ pounds ground beef

1 cup prepared ranch dressing mix (or bottled ranch dressing), divided

¾ cup seasoned breadcrumbs

¾ sweet onion, finely chopped

Salt and pepper to taste

6 sesame buns, lightly buttered and toasted

Combine ground beef with ¾ cup ranch dressing, breadcrumbs, and onion. Mix gently and form into 4 to 6 patties. Sprinkle with salt and pepper.

Grill to desired temperature and serve on lightly buttered and toasted buns with a tablespoon ranch dressing and any additional toppings you love—lettuce, tomato, onion, pickles, etc.

Ground Pork Muenster Cheeseburgers

1 pound ground pork

¼ teaspoon red wine vinegar

¼ teaspoon celery seed

¼ teaspoon oregano

2 tablespoons Dijon mustard

Garlic powder to taste

Salt and pepper to taste

4 slices Muenster cheese

4 hamburger buns

Mix together everything except cheese slices. Form gently into 4 equal-sized burgers. Grill over medium-high heat.

Top with Muenster cheese before removing from grill. Serve on heated buns with your choice of toppings.

Serious Grilling

Pineapple Spam Bacon Swiss Burger

I've been making use of SPAM since I was a college student. This recipe is twenty years in the making. The salty meat flavor of SPAM combines perfectly with the sweetness of grilled pineapple. Add bacon and Swiss cheese and you have one heck of a good burger.

1 (8-ounce) can sliced pineapple, juice reserved

2 to 3 tablespoons teriyaki sauce

½ cup yellow mustard

1 (12-ounce) can SPAM, sliced

½ onion, sliced

4 slices Swiss cheese

8 bacon slices, cooked crisp

4 artisan hamburger buns

Drain pineapple, reserving juice. Combine teriyaki sauce, mustard and 2 tablespoons pineapple juice in a bowl. Coat SPAM slices with teriyaki mixture and grill just until heated through.

Grill pineapple and onion slices until hot. Stack a slice of pineapple on a slice of SPAM and cover with onions and a slice of Swiss cheese. Continue grilling until cheese is melted. Top with bacon.

Serve hot on a bun with your choice of additional toppings.

SPAM was introduced in 1937 and gained popularity during World War II. No one really knows the true meaning of the name, which might explain why it earned the nickname of "mystery meat."

Apple Butter Pork and Cheddar Burgers

1 pound lean ground pork

1 cup apple butter, divided

¼ cup chopped green onions

½ teaspoon dried thyme

½ teaspoon salt

½ teaspoon black pepper

4 ounces sliced Cheddar cheese

4 hamburger buns

Combine pork, ¾ cup apple butter, green onions, thyme, salt and pepper in a bowl. Form into 4 equal-sized patties.

Grill each burger over medium-high heat about 4 minutes on each side or until an instant-read thermometer reads 160°. Baste lightly with remaining apple butter before removing from grill.

Top with Cheddar cheese and continue to cook until cheese is melted. Serve up on your choice of bun with desired toppings.

You can also toss in a handful of finely chopped apples into the burger mix for some added flavor. Don't add too many, as it may cause your burger to break up. Flip the burgers on the grill as gently as possible.

Serious Grilling

Pork Burgers with Sweet Apricot Mayonnaise

This Apricot Mayonnaise is so good, you'll undoubtedly use it with other dishes.

1½ pounds ground pork

¼ cup minced sweet onion

½ tablespoon dried cilantro

½ teaspoon seasoned salt

4 to 6 potato bread buns

Spring mix lettuce

4 to 6 thick tomato slices

Apricot Mayonnaise

APRICOT MAYONNAISE:

½ cup apricot preserves

½ cup mayonnaise

½ tablespoon lemon juice

2 teaspoons dried cilantro

Dash of chili powder

Combine pork, onion, cilantro and seasoned salt in a bowl; form into 4 to 6 equal-sized burgers.

Cook on a medium-high heat grill to an internal temperature of 160°.

Toast buns lightly on grill. Build burgers with fresh spring mix lettuce, a thick slice of tomato and Apricot Mayonnaise.

For Mayonnaise: Combine all ingredients in a bowl and mix well. Refrigerate until burgers are ready to serve.

Spicy Asian Ground Pork Burgers with Yum Yum Sauce

Have you ever been to a Japanese steakhouse and overloaded on the white sauce? This sauce, commonly called Yum Yum Sauce, is the perfect addition to this Japanese steakhouse-inspired ground pork burger.

1½ pounds ground pork

2 teaspoons minced garlic

1 tablespoon hot Asian mustard

½ tablespoon ginger

2 tablespoons soy sauce

4 to 6 grilled zucchini slices

4 to 6 grilled onion slices

Olive oil

Salt and pepper to taste

4 to 6 hamburger buns

Yum Yum Sauce

YUM YUM SAUCE:

½ cup plain Greek yogurt (or sour cream)

½ cup mayonnaise

½ tablespoon butter, melted

½ tablespoon unseasoned rice wine vinegar

½ tablespoon milk

½ tablespoon ketchup

½ tablespoon sugar

¼ tablespoon garlic powder

Dash paprika

Dash cayenne

Mix together first 5 ingredients and form into 4 to 6 burgers.

Grill over medium-high heat 10 to 12 minutes, turning once. Cook until an instant-read thermometer reads 160°.

About halfway through the grilling process, lightly brush zucchini and onion slices with olive oil and place on grill. (Use a grilling basket or foil if needed.) Sprinkle with a little salt and pepper.

Serve burgers on buns topped with grilled zucchini and onion slices and topped with Yum Yum Sauce.

For Sauce: Combine all ingredients in a bowl and chill before serving.

I've made the Yum Yum Sauce using plain fat-free Greek yogurt, as well as with fat-free sour cream and light mayonnaise. I've also it made using all mayonnaise or all sour cream. All have turned out well.

Serious Grilling

Ground Pork BLT Burgers

I'm a big fan of a classic BLT served on white bread. So, why not bring that flavor to a ground pork burger?

1 pound ground pork

6 bacon slices, cooked and crumbled (plus more for topping, if desired)

Salt and pepper to taste

Garlic powder to taste

Mayonnaise

8 slices bread

Lettuce

4 tomato slices

Mix ground pork, bacon, salt, pepper and garlic powder in a bowl and shape into 4 patties.

Grill or broil 4 minutes on each side or until done; place on paper towels for a few minutes to drain.

Spread mayonnaise on untoasted bread. Top with lettuce, tomato and more bacon slices, if desired.

Try adding chopped cucumbers, dill and garlic to the mayonnaise for an easy tzatziki spread.

Hearty Ground Pork and Mushroom Burger

½ cup finely chopped mushrooms

¼ cup chopped onion

2 teaspoons butter

1½ pounds ground pork

Salt and pepper to taste

1 garlic clove, minced

2 tablespoons steak sauce

Sauté mushrooms and onion in a skillet with butter. When soft, remove from heat and combine with ground pork in a bowl. Add salt, pepper, garlic and steak sauce. Form into 6 equal-sized burgers.

Place patties on grill over medium-hot heat and cook 10 to 15 minutes, turning as few times as possible to limit breaking.

HOLD THE KETCHUP

Louis Lassen is well-known as inventor of the hamburger and for his iconic restaurant, Louis' Lunch in New Haven, Connecticut. Jeff Lassen, great grandson of Lassen, let me know that there are a few fun rules when it comes to what you can get as a condiment…and ketchup is not an option! "It's a long standing tradition," Jeff said with a smile. "We pride ourselves on quality meats, great hamburgers, and toppings that we feel match our burgers. You don't need to cover a Louis Lunch hamburger with a bunch of stuff that covers up great flavor." Rumors are that when Yale students try to sneak in some ketchup they are politely asked to leave. "It's part of the history and lore of Louis Lunch," Jeff said laughing. "We welcome every customer with open arms and they can have their burgers anyway they want them… as long as they don't want ketchup!"

Gyro Burgers with Cucumber Sour Cream Sauce

If you enjoy a nice gyro sandwich on fresh pita bread, then you'll enjoy this Gyro Burger made with ground lamb and a chilled Cucumber Sour Cream Sauce.

1 pound ground lamb

½ teaspoon mint

1 tablespoon dried cilantro

1 tablespoon oregano

1 tablespoon minced garlic

2 teaspoons cumin powder

1 teaspoon white wine vinegar

1 teaspoon allspice

1 teaspoon red pepper flakes

Salt and pepper to taste

2 pita breads

Feta cheese

Shredded lettuce

Chopped tomato

Finely sliced onion

CUCUMBER SOUR CREAM SAUCE:

1 cup sour cream

⅔ cup peeled and finely chopped cucumber

1 teaspoon minced garlic

1 teaspoon dill

1 teaspoon prepared mustard

½ teaspoon garlic powder

Dash black pepper

Combine lamb, mint, cilantro, oregano, minced garlic, cumin, vinegar, allspice, red pepper, salt and pepper in a bowl; mix. Gently form 4 burgers.

Cook on preheated medium-high grill using direct heat, turning 1 or 2 times.

Serve burgers hot in a warmed half piece of pita bread with feta cheese, Cucumber Sour Cream Sauce, lettuce, tomato and onion.

For Sauce: Combine in a bowl and refrigerate at least 1 hour before serving.

Ground Buffalo Double Cheeseburgers with Chili Lime Mayo

You may have confused buffalo and bison — I know I did for years. According to the National Bison Association, it's a common mistake. The term "buffalo" is scientifically incorrect for the North American species. Common usage has made the term "buffalo" an acceptable synonym for the American bison.

1 pound ground bison

½ pound ground breakfast sausage (or ground Italian sausage)

2 tablespoons Dijon mustard

Salt and pepper to taste

Onion slices, grilled

Mushrooms, sliced and grilled

Melted butter

4 hamburger buns

8 slices Swiss cheese

CHILI LIME MAYO:

½ cup mayonnaise

1 tablespoon chili powder

½ tablespoon lime juice

Dash red pepper flakes

Combine bison meat, ground sausage, Dijon mustard, salt and pepper in a bowl and mix loosely. (Don't overwork the meat.) Form into 8 thin and wide patties. Grill over high heat 3 to 4 minutes per side or until cooked through. When the burgers are finished, remove from grill to rest a few minutes.

Grill onions and mushrooms alongside burgers using a grilling tray or on foil. Brush with melted butter.

Build burgers on 4 buns with 2 slices of cheese per sandwich. Top with grilled onions and mushrooms plus your favorite toppings. Serve immediately.

For Mayonnaise: Combine all ingredients in a bowl and mix well. Cover and chill slightly before serving.

NOTE: The lime juice will break down the mayonnaise so only prepare as much as you can use for your meal. If you have leftovers, cover and keep in the fridge for only 1 day.

Serious Grilling

Black and White Bean Swiss Cheeseburgers

This is my favorite veggie burger.

1 (15-ounce) can black beans, drained and rinsed

1 (15-ounce) can Great Northern beans, drained and rinsed

½ cup finely chopped onion

3 tablespoons mayonnaise

½ cup plain dry breadcrumbs

2 teaspoons ground cumin powder

1 teaspoon chili powder

1 teaspoon cayenne

½ tablespoon dried cilantro

Salt and pepper to taste

4 slices Swiss cheese

4 poppy seed or sesame seed hamburger buns

Combine everything, except cheese and buns, in a food processor and pulse just enough to break up beans. (Do not over-process as you don't want to liquefy your beans.) Form into 4 equal-sized portions, adding additional breadcrumbs if needed.

Place each burger on a coated square of foil and then place on a preheated medium-high grill. Cook 4 to 5 minutes on 1 side.

Gently turn burgers over and peel foil away gently. Cook an additional 3 to 4 minutes, top with cheese and serve hot on bun.

Big Time Burgers

Easy Grilled Salmon Burgers with Sweet Relish Tartar Sauce

These burgers can be made with fresh salmon, but using canned salmon is simple and quick and still tastes great. My grandfather Campbell used to make this recipe during World War II to stretch meals. My mom often said he would save the juice from the can and use it later, or add so many crackers that she was "never sure if we were eating salmon patties or salmon-flavored cracker patties."

1 (15-ounce) can red salmon, drained and checked for bones

⅓ cup dry Italian breadcrumbs

2 tablespoons minced green bell pepper

3 tablespoons mayonnaise

1 tablespoon lemon juice

1 egg, beaten

Dash garlic powder

Salt and pepper to taste

SWEET RELISH TARTAR SAUCE:

½ cup mayonnaise

1 tablespoon sweet pickle relish

½ teaspoon Creole seasoning

Dash chili powder

1 teaspoon lemon or lime juice

1 to 3 drops hot sauce

In a bowl, break up salmon, discarding any small bones. Add in remaining ingredients and form into 2 patties.

Place patties on squares of foil prepped with nonstick spray. Chill about 30 minutes to help burger set.

Place burgers (with foil underneath) onto a medium heated grill grate and cook until burger is firm. Turn and cook other side and gently peel foil back to remove. You can also cook on a grilling tray or side burner in a skillet.

Serve up on your choice of bun with fresh tomato slices, lettuce, onions, and Sweet Relish Tartar Sauce.

For Sauce: Combine in a bowl and chill before serving.

Serious Grilling

Italian Parmesan Turkey Burgers with Grilled Tomatoes

The trick to this recipe is to use shredded Parmesan cheese instead of the dried and grated style found on the table at most pizza restaurants.

1 pound ground turkey

½ cup shredded Parmesan cheese

1½ tablespoons Italian seasoning

½ tablespoon parsley

2 teaspoons thyme

4 tomato slices

4 onion slices

Olive oil

Salt and pepper to taste

4 hamburger buns

In a bowl, mix ground turkey, cheese, seasoning, parsley and thyme. Form into 4 equal-sized burgers and grill over medium-high heat. Cook patties 12 to 15 minutes or until thermometer inserted in center reads 165°.

While burgers are cooking, drizzle tomato and onion slices with olive oil and sprinkle with a small dash of salt and pepper. Grill over high heat on coated grates, or in a grilling basket, until edges are browned.

Serve patties hot on your choice of bun with tomatoes and onions.

Note: Lean ground turkey may benefit from the addition of an egg, or egg white, as a binding agent. Ground turkey with a higher fat content may benefit from the addition of seasoned breadcrumbs.

PIGGING OUT PORK

PORK IS THE KING OF SOUTHERN BARBECUE.

Growing up in the South, I thought barbecue was all hickory pit slow-smoked pork...until I was about 18 years old. That's when I ordered the "Large Sandwich Combo" at a barbecue joint. It was a simple order...until I was asked if I wanted "pork or beef?" My mind raced through the possibilities. Well, by golly, my eyes were opened. I discovered barbecue can be just about anything and I set out to try as many types as I could. However, this section is dedicated to the king of barbecue - pork. (Ribs are in the Rib Section.)

Pork should be cooked thoroughly. Use a meat thermometer to judge doneness. Here's the breakdown.

- 145° safe internal temp for most pork — chops, steaks, etc. using a GRILL.

- 195° to 205° for Boston butt - slow smoked or offset grilled using LOW AND SLOW METHOD (next page).

After you take your pork off the grill, let it rest 10 minutes. If you cut into it right away, all juices will run out. Resting allows the juices to redistribute into the meat to keep it moist.

Serious Grilling

Boston Butt Basics

Offset grilling or smoking a pork Boston butt is really pretty easy. That's where the secret of "low-and-slow" comes in - maintaining a constant low temperature with slow cooking times. If you cook tough meat such as Boston butts and ribs too fast at too high of a temperature, then you'll end up with an even tougher piece of meat. Cooking "low-and-slow" produces a juicy and tender finished product.

Offset Grilling or Smoking? There are huge differences between offset grilling on a covered grill and using a barbecue smoker. A **smoker** is most often two chambers, with one chamber dedicated to the heat source and smoke and a larger chamber dedicated to holding the meat. The end result is a lower maintained temperature that cooks the meat slower without too much risk of burning. A **covered grill** is one chamber, with the heat source below and the meat directly above the heat on grates. Simply put, build your heat source on one side of the grill and put the meat on the other side. For round grills, place the heat source in a ring around the outside wall of the grill. You can control heat and air flow using vents.

• Cook your Boston butt on the grill, smoker, or even in the oven at a maintained temperature between 220° and 250° for 1½ to 2 hours per pound. The air temperature outside, wind and moisture can all affect your cooking time. Cook times may also differ due to the size and shape of the meat, how much fat it has and even the age. For this reason, the 1 ½ hour per pound cooking time is really just a rough idea. Always cook to your desired internal temperature checked using an instant-read thermometer.

• Sliced or chopped should hit an internal temperature between 180° and 190°.

• Pulled Boston butts should hit an internal temperature between 195° and 205° before it is tender enough to easily pull apart.

The Internal Temperature Stall: When I started smoking Boston butts I was baffled by what I now know is the "stall"—when a slow-smoked Boston butt hits an internal temperature of around 170° to 180° then stops rising. At that point, too many people pull the butts off the smoker and the meat suffers in taste and tenderness. What's happening is that much of the fat is beginning to render off. Don't worry, after a short period of time, the internal temp will begin to rise. Or you can use the optional "Foil Wrap Method" by wrapping the butt in several layers of foil to increase internal temp to 205° to 220°, creating a flavor-packed tender Boston butt suitable for pulled pork.

• Allow Boston butt to rest several minutes before pulling, slicing or chopping.

Carolina-Style Pulled Pork

Jason from Hickory, North Carolina, says hickory-smoked Carolina pork barbecue requires apple cider vinegar, lots of smoke and plenty of time plus a thin barbecue sauce to finish things off.

1 pork butt (shoulder)

¼ cup hot sauce

1 gallon apple cider vinegar

1 tablespoon crushed red pepper

1¼ cups Worcestershire sauce

Your favorite barbecue rub or Basic Deck Chef Rub (page 237)

Carolina Vinegar Sauce (page 246)

Place pork butt in a deep bowl. Combine hot sauce, vinegar, red pepper and Worcestershire; pour over pork and marinate several hours in refrigerator (overnight is best).

Remove pork and boil marinade to use as a basting sauce. Cook pork long and slow using indirect heat over a hickory wood fire to an internal temperature of 220°, about 1½ hours per pound.

Pull with a fork and serve with Carolina Vinegar Sauce.

Serious Grilling

Kent's Pineapple Mustard Marinated and Rubbed Boston Butt

This is my basic method for smoking a Boston butt. I've done this on smokers of all types, in a grill using the offset method, and even finished up in an oven when lightning storms hit the area and I didn't think standing by a big metal thing in the back yard was such good idea. The basic lesson that I can pass on about low-and-slow cooking is keep it simple and let the low temps, grilling flavor and smoke from wood or wood chips do the talking.

1 Boston butt

2 to 3 tablespoons pineapple juice (or orange juice)

½ cup mustard

½ tablespoon oil

½ cup Basic Deck Chef Rub (page 237)

Place meat in a large bowl or baking dish. Combine juice, mustard and oil in a bowl and brush over meat. Allow it to rest while you make your rub.

Rub the heck out of your Boston butt with your rub. Cover bowl well with cling wrap and place in fridge about 6 hours or overnight if possible.

Set up your covered smoker (or covered grill for indirect heat) at about 225° to 250°. To maintain this temp have plenty of charcoal (or gas) and wood chips on hand.

Place butt in smoker and smoke to an internal temp of 205° for pulled pork, a bit less for sliced or chopped pork butt. Cooking time may vary between 1½ to 2 hours per pound. Be sure to check with a meat thermometer.

Allow butt to rest several minutes before pulling, slicing or chopping.

THE MAIN RULE: Keep the lid closed as much as possible and keep an eye on maintaining your heat.

Limoncello Grilled Pork Roast

1 (3- to 4-pound) pork roast

½ cup limoncello

1 tablespoon minced garlic

1 tablespoon minced onion

3 teaspoons rosemary

3 teaspoons thyme

Parsley flakes

Salt and pepper to taste

LIMONCELLO SAUCE:

1 cup ketchup

½ cup yellow mustard

¼ cup minced onion

¼ cup minced red bell pepper

¼ cup Worcestershire sauce

¼ cup limoncello

½ tablespoon brown sugar

Salt and pepper to taste

Place pork roast in a large heavy-duty zip-close bag. Combine limoncello with garlic and onion; pour over roast. Chill 2 to 3 hours.

Remove pork roast from marinade and rub with rosemary, thyme, parsley, salt and pepper.

Grill on a preheated medium-high grill, turning as needed. Keep grill lid closed as much as possible. About halfway through grilling process, remove pork roast from direct heat and place on several sheets of aluminum foil. Gently pour some of the remaining marinade over pork and wrap tightly.

Finish grilling process on an upper rack, turning as needed. Grill to an internal temperature of 140°. Rest roast several minutes before slicing. Serve with Limoncello Sauce on the side.

For Sauce: Combine all ingredients in a saucepan and simmer over medium heat until vegetables are soft. Serve warm.

Serious Grilling

Red Wine Marinated Pork Tenderloin

Grab a bottle of your favorite red wine and sip it while you're grilling up this tasty pork tenderloin.

1 pork tenderloin

2 cups red wine, divided

Salt and pepper to taste

2 tablespoons oil

½ onion, chopped

1 cup chopped mushrooms

Minced garlic

2 tablespoons barbecue sauce (or mustard)

Place tenderloin in a large zip-close bag with 1 cup red wine. Add salt and pepper to taste. Remove as much air as possible before sealing. Turn bag several times to fully coat tenderloin. Refrigerate overnight, turning occasionally.

Add oil to a large heated skillet. Add tenderloin, onion, mushrooms and garlic. Brown tenderloin on each side just enough to give the outside a nice seared look; do not fully cook. Remove tenderloin from skillet (reserving onion and mushrooms) and wrap several times in foil.

Finish cooking on the upper rack of grill over medium-low heat. Close lid and grill to an internal temperature of 140° to 145°.

While tenderloin is grilling, add 1 cup red wine and barbecue sauce to skillet with onions and mushrooms; bring to a boil. Boil 5 minutes; simmer over low heat until tenderloin is ready. Serve tenderloin with sauce.

Serious Grilling

Fruity Wine Marinated Pineapple Pork Tenderloin

Use a fruit-flavored wine, or even a wine cooler, as a marinade for your next pork tenderloin. Add in some pineapple chunks and a few spices and you're good to go for a tasty twist on your next grilled tenderloin.

1 pork tenderloin

1¼ cups citrus-flavored wine (or wine cooler), divided

1 (8-ounce) can crushed pineapple, reserve juice

1 cup barbecue sauce

⅓ cup minced onion

2 tablespoons mustard

Place tenderloin in a glass baking dish along with 1 cup wine and drained pineapple. Cover and chill several hours or overnight. (Refrigerate reserved pineapple juice to use in sauce.)

Spoon about ½ cup pineapple pieces from marinade.

Preheat grill to medium-high heat and brush grates with vegetable oil. Place tenderloin on grill and close cover. Grill the tenderloin until it reaches an internal temperature of 140°. Allow tenderloin to rest for a few minutes before slicing.

While tenderloin is cooking, combine reserved juice from pineapple, remaining ¼ cup wine, barbecue sauce, minced onion and mustard in a saucepan. Add the ½ cup pineapple from marinade. Cover and simmer over medium-low heat (on stove or side-burner) while tenderloin is grilling.

Serve sliced tenderloin topped with sauce.

PORK CHOP VERSION: Substitute thick boneless pork chops for the tenderloin. When done, serve on buttered and grilled Texas toast with sauce drizzled over the top for a tasty open-faced pork chop sandwich.

CRAZY SIMPLE GRILLED PORK RECIPES

Here are three crazy simple recipes for grilled pork. They are great to fix when you are in a hurry to get dinner ready — choose your pork cut and then fire up the grill.

Teriyaki and Sweet Onion Grilled Pork Tenderloin

1 pork tenderloin

Vegetable oil

Salt and pepper to taste

½ cup soy sauce

2 tablespoons brown sugar

Garlic powder to taste

1 sweet onion, thinly sliced

Rub pork tenderloin lightly with oil, salt and pepper.

Combine soy sauce, brown sugar and garlic powder in a small bowl. Place tenderloin, onion and soy sauce mixture in a covered glass bowl (or zip-close bag). Chill 2 to 3 hours or overnight.

Remove tenderloin (reserving sauce and onion); grill over high heat 5 minutes each side to brown outside. Place tenderloin on several sheets of heavy-duty foil and cover with reserved onion slices and sauce. Wrap tightly and finish grilling over medium heat or on an upper rack to an internal temperature of 145°.

Serious Grilling

Spicy Apricot Pork Steaks

4 pork steaks

Salt and pepper to taste

Basic Deck Chef Rub
  (page 237)

Hot sauce

1 cup apricot preserves,
  heated

Rub steaks with salt, pepper and rub. Grill over medium-high heat to an internal temperature of 145°. Brush each pork steak with hot sauce and heated apricot preserves before removing from grill.

Orange and Chili Rubbed Bone-In Pork Chops

4 bone-in pork chops

2 cups orange juice

2 tablespoons vegetable oil

2 tablespoons chili powder

Dash cumin powder

Dash garlic salt

Marinate chops in orange juice several hours. Remove from juice and brush with oil. Combine chili powder, cumin and garlic salt; rub over chops. Grill over medium-high heat to an internal temperature of 145°.

Peach and Whiskey Glazed Red Wine Pork Chops

6 (½-inch-thick) pork steaks

Salt and pepper to taste

¼ cup red wine

WHISKEY PEACH GLAZE:

2 tablespoons oil

½ small sweet onion, diced

1 (29-ounce) can sliced
  peaches

⅔ cups whiskey

2 tablespoons brown sugar

2 teaspoons balsamic vinegar

½ stick butter

Place pork in a glass baking dish or zip-close bag. Add salt, pepper and red wine. Coat evenly, cover or seal and chill 2 to 3 hours.

Grill over medium-high heat, turning as needed, to an internal temperature of 140°. Brush heavily with Whiskey Peach Glaze before removing from grill.

Top each chop with a slice of peach from glaze.

For Glaze: Heat oil in a skillet over medium heat. Add onion and peaches with half the juice from the can. Simmer about 5 minutes; add whiskey, brown sugar, vinegar and butter. Continue cooking, stirring, until butter is melted, onions are very tender and sauce is well mixed.

Onion Soup Pork Chops

Tailgate Friendly

4 to 6 (½-inch-thick) pork
  chops

3 tablespoons oil

1 (2-ounce) packet onion soup
  mix

1 tablespoon soy sauce

½ lime, juiced

Place chops in a zip-close bag or glass baking dish and drizzle with oil. Top with onion soup mix, soy sauce and lime juice. Make sure chops are evenly coated. Seal bag or cover baking dish and chill several hours.

Place chops on a medium-high heat; grill with wood chunks of your choice.

Grill chops, turning once or twice, to an internal temperature of 140°.

Serious Grilling

Chuck Wagon Coffee Bourbon Pork Chops

During old-time cattle drives in the American West, chuck wagon cooks were innovators in simple recipes packed with flavor using few ingredients and little waste. A common ingredient was leftover coffee. I've seen it included in recipes for everything from chili to brownies. So, why not use it with pork chops?

1½ cups brewed coffee

⅓ cup maple syrup

⅓ cup ketchup

2 tablespoons bourbon

2 tablespoons cider vinegar

2 tablespoons mustard

2 garlic cloves, minced

Salt and pepper to taste

4 pork chops, 1 inch thick

In a large bowl, combine all ingredients, except pork chops, and mix well. Place pork chops in a glass baking dish and top with the marinade. Lift each pork chop to coat evenly. Cover and chill overnight, turning a couple of times to evenly marinate.

Remove pork chops from marinade and boil marinade in a saucepan several minutes before using as a baste.

Grill pork chops on a preheated grill over medium-high heat about 5 minutes per side, basting with cooked marinade.

Teriyaki Barbecue Pork Chops

8 boneless pork chops

Salt and pepper to taste

Garlic powder to taste

½ tablespoon hot sauce

½ teaspoon crushed red pepper

½ cup teriyaki sauce

1 cup barbecue sauce

2 tablespoons Worcestershire sauce

Place pork chops in a glass baking dish. Season with salt, pepper, garlic powder, hot sauce and crushed red pepper. Carefully brush with teriyaki sauce; cover and chill several hours.

Before grilling, combine barbecue sauce and Worcestershire and baste over chops. Grill over medium-high heat, turning as needed, until done.

Serve hot with your choice of sides, over rice or vegetables or on a toasted hoagie bun.

STUFFED VERSION:
If you get some thick chops, butterfly cut them and grill stuffed with your choice of seasoned vegetables. Just be sure to baste the inside of the chops as well.

Serious Grilling

Margarita Pork Chops with Sweet Onion Sauce

1 pound pork chops

1 cup liquid margarita drink mix

1 teaspoon cumin

1 clove garlic, minced

2 tablespoons butter

2 teaspoons lime juice

1 teaspoon sugar

SWEET ONION SAUCE/SALSA:

This is actually two recipes in one. Place it in a blender for a sauce or leave it chunky for a salsa. It's your choice.

3 cups diced fresh tomatoes

2 cups diced sweet onions

1 jalapeño, seeded and diced

1 tablespoon minced garlic

1½ tablespoons chopped cilantro

½ tablespoon chopped parsley

2 teaspoons sugar

2 teaspoons salt

2 tablespoons white vinegar

2 tablespoons fresh lime juice

Combine all ingredients in a zip-close bag (or glass baking dish). Coat chops evenly and seal bag (or cover dish). Marinate 2 hours in refrigerator.

Grill over high heat, turning as needed, to an internal temperature of 140°.

Serve hot with Sweet Onion Sauce/Salsa.

For Sauce: Combine all sauce/salsa ingredients in bowl, cover and chill about an hour. Purée in blender with 1 tablespoon water and heat slightly in a microwave. Drizzle over finished chops.

For Salsa: Skip the blender and microwave; use as a topping for finished chops.

Apple Butter Pork Chops with Reduced Double Cola & Pecan Sauce

Double Cola in Chattanooga, Tennessee, was one of the smaller sponsors for the Hixson Motorsports Team (Soddy Daisy, Tennessee) during the time I was hanging out with them for the ARCA Racing Series. It seems Double Cola provided beverages for the mostly volunteer crew on race weekends, and one of the crew used Double Cola to make a sweet and thick barbecue sauce. I couldn't wait for the chance to use Double Cola in a recipe of my own.

4 pork chops

1 cup apple butter

2 tablespoons butter

½ cup finely chopped pecans

2 cups chopped apples

1 (12-ounce) can Double cola (or any other cola, but not diet)

Hot sauce

Coat pork chops with apple butter; cover and chill 2 hours or longer.

Grill pork chops over medium heat until done.

While chops are cooking on the grill, use your side burner (or cook inside on the stove) to heat butter in a skillet. Add pecans and apples and sauté about 5 minutes (just enough to get some color on the apples).

Add cola slowly; it will foam up a bit so go carefully. Add a few dashes of hot sauce and allow mixture to reduce by a third.

Serve pork chops topped with sauce.

DOUBLE QUENCH
Double-Cola earned its name because its 12-ounce bottles were twice the size of other soda bottles being sold at the time.

Serious Grilling

Ginger Lemon Thai Pork Chops with Plum Sauce

3 tablespoons soy sauce

3 tablespoons honey

1 tablespoon rice wine vinegar

1 tablespoon lemon juice

1 tablespoon olive oil

3 garlic cloves, minced

1 tablespoon minced garlic

3 teaspoons ground ginger

4 bone-in pork chops

PLUM SAUCE:

½ (16-ounce) jar plum jam or jelly (1 cup)

2 tablespoons vinegar

2 tablespoons water

1 tablespoon melted butter

1 tablespoon brown sugar

1 tablespoon dried minced onion

1 teaspoon crushed red pepper flakes

1 garlic clove, minced

2 teaspoons soy sauce

½ teaspoon ground ginger

Combine all ingredients, except pork chops, in a bowl and mix well.

Place pork chops in a glass baking dish and coat evenly with marinade. Chill while preparing Plum Sauce and preheating grill.

Grill over medium high-heat, turning as needed, to an internal temperature of 145°. Serve warm with Plum Sauce.

For Sauce: Combine all ingredients in a saucepan and heat until jam melts. Serve warm with pork chops.

Serious Grilling

Spicy Alabama White Sauce Grilled Pork Steaks

Tailgate Friendly

4 to 6 pork steaks

Salt and pepper to taste

2 cups mayonnaise

⅓ cup water

⅓ cup apple cider vinegar

½ tablespoon black pepper

1½ tablespoons hot sauce

½ tablespoon mustard

2 teaspoons salt

2 teaspoons sugar

2 teaspoons minced garlic

Season pork steaks with salt and pepper; set aside.

Combine remaining ingredients in a bowl; mix well. Place half the sauce in a covered container, add pork and refrigerate overnight. Refrigerate remaining sauce separately in a covered bowl.

Heat grill to high heat. Remove chops, discarding marinade. Grill, turning once or twice, until cooked to an internal temperature of 140°. Serve with reserved sauce.

PIGS ON WALL STREET

Free-roaming hogs were famous for rampaging through the valuable grain fields of colonial New York City farmers. The Manhattan Island residents chose to block the troublesome hogs with a long, permanent wall on the northern edge of what is now Lower Manhattan. A street was built along the wall… "Wall Street!"

Source: Illinois Pork Producers Association / National Pork Board

Hickory-Smoked Coca-Cola Ham

1 half ham with bone

1 (2-liter) bottle Coca-Cola

Salt and pepper to taste

Basic Deck Chef Rub
(page 237)

FINISHING GLAZE:

1 (12-ounce) can Coca-Cola

2 tablespoons butter

½ cup orange marmalade

Score ham in an x pattern all over, about ¼ inch deep (or buy a spiral sliced ham). Place ham in a large bowl or stockpot; pour cola over ham. Season to taste with salt and pepper. Cover and place in fridge overnight or as long as possible, turning a couple of times.

Set up your covered grill for indirect grilling with hickory wood chips, with a drip pan, at about 350°.

Remove ham from cola and rub liberally with seasoning rub. Place ham on grates over a drip pan and grill 16 to 18 minutes per pound to an internal temperature of 140°. During last 10 minutes of grilling, baste ham with Finishing Glaze and continue cooking with grill cover closed.

For Glaze: Heat a deep-sided skillet; carefully add cola and butter. Cook, stirring, over medium-high heat until slightly reduced. Add marmalade and mix well. Remove from heat.

PORK & "UNCLE SAM"

There are many claims of the origin of "Uncle Sam." One of them includes Samuel Wilson who was a meat-packer from Troy, New York. During the war of 1812, Wilson was said to have shipped a boat load of pork to U.S. troops. Each barrel was reported to have been stamped with "U.S." which showed clearly while unloaded on the docks and when shipped to troops. Legend has it that the U.S. military men began to say that the "U.S." stood for Samuel—like being a good uncle – or as…"Uncle Sam."

Source: Illinois Pork Producers Association / National Pork Board

Serious Grilling

Grilled Ham Steaks
for Breakfast or Brunch

A thick-cut ham steak perfect for breakfast or brunch.

4 to 6 bone-in breakfast ham steaks

1 stick butter, melted

⅓ cup orange juice

1 tablespoon brown sugar

Dash cinnamon

Dash salt and pepper

Lay ham steaks in a single layer on a baking sheet. Combine melted butter and orange juice in a bowl; stir in brown sugar. Mix well and brush over steaks, coating them evenly.

Grill over medium-high heat while brushing with sauce and turning once or twice. Grill about 5 minutes on each side or to an internal temperature of 140°.

Sprinkle lightly with cinnamon, salt and pepper to taste. Serve hot as a breakfast or brunch item.

Grilled Ham Steaks
for Lunch or Dinner

It's amazing how much this recipe changes with only a slight difference in ingredients; this hearty recipe is perfect for lunch or dinner.

4 to 6 bone-in breakfast ham steaks

1 stick butter, melted

⅓ cup steak sauce

1 tablespoon brown sugar

Dash salt and pepper

Lay ham steaks in a single layer on a baking sheet. Combine melted butter and steak sauce in a bowl; stir in brown sugar. Mix well and brush over steaks, coating them evenly.

Grill over medium-high heat while brushing with sauce and turning once or twice. Grill about 5 minutes on each side or to an internal temperature of 140°.

Sprinkle with salt and pepper to taste. Serve hot with your choice of sides.

RACK UP THE RIBS

SOME BASIC RIB TECHNIQUES

TRIM AND SCORE MEMBRANE: The first thing you should do is trim any large pieces of excess fat or bone. Then score or remove the membrane on the underside of the ribs.

RUB OR MARINATE: Ribs should be treated with a rub or a marinade. Rub ribs with your preferred rub or soak in a flavorful marinade, refrigerating overnight to allow the flavor to be soaked in by the meat. It's a good idea to use nonreactive containers, or even layers of cling wrap.

MOISTURE: Low-and-slow cooking is necessary to tenderize the meat, but it can suck the moisture right out. So it's always a good idea to use a drip and water pan as well as a mop sauce. A mop sauce is a thin sauce you can apply to the meat when you turn or rotate pieces.

KEEP IT COVERED: Keep the grill cover closed as much as possible to retain heat and moisture. Quickly rotate, turn, mop and check temperature whenever you open the lid.

WHEN ARE MY RIBS DONE? The rib meat will shrink back from the bones about a quarter of an inch. With just a little pull, bones should twist and pull away from the meat. There should be slight resistance and not fall completely apart.

Serious Grilling

Types of Ribs

PORK:

- **Pork Baby Back / Top Loin Ribs:** Welcome to RIB COUNTRY! These are the ribs known around the country as a barbecue favorite. You can cook these versatile ribs just about any way you want—slow smoked, indirect grilling, direct grilling, low oven baking, rotisserie and more. One rack contains 10 to 12 bones and generally feeds 2 people.

- **Back Ribs:** Back ribs originate from the blade and center section of the pork loin, which is known for the "finger meat" between the bones. Back ribs also are referred to as "baby" back ribs because they are smaller than spareribs. A rack typically weighs between 1½ and 1¾ pounds.

- **Baby Back Pork Trimmed:** These ribs are trimmed to a smaller size than the larger baby back / top loin ribs. They are popular for direct grilling, indirect grilling, and with low and slow smoker methods. The smaller rack size makes them a good meal for one person but two could split a rack if you include some sides.

- **Cut Pork Riblets:** Not to be confused with rib tips, they are generally smaller than most cuts of ribs, sometimes made up of assorted leftover rib cuts, and are often found on appetizer menus.

- **Pork Spareribs:** The popular sparerib comes from the belly of the hog and are typically larger and a little less meaty than back ribs but packed with flavor. Since these racks have tougher meat, they should be cooked using low and slow, indirect heat methods.

- **Country-Style Pork Ribs:** Country-style pork ribs are cut from the rib end of the pork loin and are the meatiest variety of ribs. They are sold as "slabs" or in individual servings. These are perfect for those who want to use a knife and fork.

- **Rib Tips:** Rib tips are the end result of trimmed spareribs. They can also be smaller pieces of trimmed ribs and generally contain cartilage-style ribs rather than hard bones.

BEEF RIBS:

- **Beef Back Ribs:** Beef back ribs are the standard rack of beef ribs. They are great for grilling or broiling. Beef back ribs are also known as beef rib bones, beef riblets, and beef finger ribs depending on the cut.

- **Beef Short Ribs:** Also known as boneless braising ribs, English short ribs, and beef middle ribs, beef short ribs are generally uniform-sized boneless cuts, suited for braising and some low-and-slow offset grilling.

Kent's Easy Grilled Pork Barbecue Ribs

There are no secret ingredients here. This is more a grilling method than a recipe. Whenever I demonstrate this, I use ingredients from local stores. The brands vary but the results are always delicious. Follow the directions as closely as possible — your temp and times may vary on your own grill.

2 slabs pork ribs

2 cups pre-prepared marinade

1 (1.6-ounce) packet BBQ pulled pork seasoning

Remove back membrane from underside of ribs. Lightly coat with marinade and rub with seasoning. (Reserve remaining marinade and seasoning.) Tightly wrap ribs in plastic wrap (or place in a covered pan) and store in fridge overnight.

Remove wrap and lightly sear both sides on grill over high heat, just enough to brown both sides, 10 to 15 minutes per side.

Remove from heat and carefully drizzle with a small amount of reserved marinade and add remaining seasoning. Wrap tightly in several layers of foil.

Reduce the heat of the grill, around 275° to 300° with the lid closed, and cook foil-wrapped ribs, with the cover down, for 2 to 3 hours, turning every 15 minutes. Use tongs and gloves to turn. You will see grease beginning to pour out as fat and connective tissue break down.

Remove meat from heat and allow to rest about 5 minutes before cutting. Baste in sauce before serving, if desired.

GRILLED RIB TIP: Ribs will start off stiff in the foil but become very limber when finished.

Serious Grilling

Holy Trinity Cajun Grilled Pork Back Mini Slabs

The "Holy Trinity" of Cajun cooking is onion, bell pepper and celery. We have all three covered here with the celery being a spice.

2 slabs pork back ribs

1 stick butter

½ cup minced bell pepper
(about 1 pepper)

½ cup minced sweet onion

2 tablespoons paprika

2 tablespoons Cajun seasoning

½ tablespoon onion powder

2 teaspoons salt

2 teaspoons onion powder

2 teaspoons black pepper

2 teaspoons oregano

2 teaspoons celery powder

Cut each slab into 3 equal-sized pieces and place on a cookie sheet. Melt butter in a skillet and sauté bell pepper and onion; remove from heat. Add remaining spices and stir to mix well. Brush butter rub evenly over each rib. Cover lightly with foil and chill overnight, or several hours.

Place ribs on a preheated covered grill using medium-high indirect heat with wood chips. Reduce temperature if grilling directly over heat source. Grilling time may be 2 to 3 hours, depending on your grill, size of rib pieces and temperature of grill.

Keep cover closed as much as you can, but turn ribs every 20 to 30 minutes. Rotate as needed around grill to cook evenly.

Maple PBR Barbecue Pork Ribs

2 slabs pork ribs

PBR WET RUB:

½ (12-ounce) can Pabst Blue Ribbon (PBR) beer, reserve other half for Mop Sauce

½ cup maple syrup

½ cup ketchup

¼ cup mustard

2 tablespoons brown sugar

2 tablespoons paprika

1 tablespoon chili powder

1 tablespoon garlic powder

3 teaspoons cayenne pepper

3 teaspoons salt

3 teaspoons pepper

PBR MOP SAUCE:

½ (12-ounce) can Pabst Blue Ribbon beer

⅓ cup apple cider vinegar

¼ cup oil

2 tablespoons Wet Rub

1 tablespoon Worcestershire sauce

Remove or score membrane from back of ribs.

For Wet Rub: Combine rub ingredients and mix well. Massage rub generously into ribs, cover and chill overnight.

For Mop Sauce: In a covered bowl, combine Mop Sauce ingredients using remaining half of beer and 2 tablespoons wet rub; refrigerate overnight.

Place Mop Sauce in a saucepan over medium-high heat and bring to a quick boil; remove from heat.

Grill ribs over medium-high heat 15 to 20 minutes each side. Baste generously with Mop Sauce. Move ribs to an upper rack and grill another hour, with the grill covered, mopping every 15 to 20 minutes.

Next, mop ribs heavily and wrap tightly in foil. Grill using reduced heat for 2 to 2½ hours, turning and rotating several times. Just before serving, remove ribs from foil and place them over direct heat a few minutes, then brush lightly with mop sauce.

Serious Grilling

Memphis-Style Dry Rubbed Ribs

RIBS:

2 to 3 slabs pork spareribs

MEMPHIS-STYLE DRY RUB
(DOUBLE AS NEEDED):

⅔ cup smoked paprika

2 tablespoons packed dark
brown sugar

1 tablespoon allspice

6 teaspoons salt

6 teaspoons onion powder

6 teaspoons garlic powder (Not
garlic salt)

4 teaspoons celery salt

4 teaspoons black pepper

2 teaspoons cayenne pepper,
or to taste

Dash cumin powder

MEMPHIS-STYLE MOP SAUCE:

1 cup barbecue sauce

½ cup water

¼ cup beer

¼ cup water

Prep ribs by scoring (or removing) membrane from back side of ribs and trim off any large pieces of loose fat. Rub ribs down evenly with Rub and place in refrigerator overnight.

Prepare grill for offset grilling, or your smoker or pit for a maintained temperature around 225°. Grill ribs, turning as needed, with cover closed as much as possible. You will want to hold a temperature around 225° for 4 to 6 hours. Grill ribs to an internal temperature of 180° to 185°.

During the last hour of cook time, frequently sprinkle additional Rub over ribs and brush with Mop Sauce.

For the Rub: Combine all of the ingredients in a bowl, mix and set aside in a dry place. Store in a dry shaker in a dry pantry for up to a month or more.

For the Mop Sauce: Combine in a small saucepan and bring to a quick boil. Mix well.

Serious Grilling

Easy Mustard Sauce Barbecue Ribs

Stash this recipe under your "It's Like Cheating" recipe file.

2 slabs pork spareribs

2 to 3 tablespoons Worcestershire sauce

2 tablespoons meat marinade

Salt and pepper to taste

Barbecue rub

CHEATERS MUSTARD BARBECUE SAUCE:

1 cup yellow mustard

1 cup barbecue sauce

¼ cup water

Remove or score membrane from back of ribs and brush with Worcestershire sauce and meat marinade. Season with salt, pepper and rub. Cover and chill an hour or so while you prepare your grill and sauce.

You can grill or smoke using method of your choice. If you grill over direct heat just be sure to not have too high of a heat source and keep grill lid closed as much as possible. Turn and rotate as needed while brushing with sauce.

For Sauce: Combine ingredients in a bowl and mix well.

Tailgate Friendly

THE PLOCHMAN MUSTARD BARREL MAKES HISTORY

If you've eaten mustard since 1957, you've probably held Plochman mustard's familiar yellow-barrel-shaped dispenser. Moritz Plochman was an emigrant from the Kingdom of Württemberg. In 1883, Plochman purchased Chicago's Premium Mustard Mills, one of the few businesses to survive the 1871 Chicago fire, later changing the company's name to Plochman. In 1957, Plochman made condiment history by selling mustard in the now famous yellow squeeze barrel. So, why is this condiment history? It was the first successful squeeze condiment in the United States.

ARCA Racing Pork Board Pork Ribs

While covering races in the ARCA Racing Series, I met some great people from the National Pork Board, which was sponsoring ARCA Champion Frank Kimmel. Before you know it, I was handing out plates to a massive number of people visiting Frank's hauler for a sandwich. Frank has moved on to another team and the Pork Board moved on from their massive Kimmel Garage Area Barbecues...sadly, the garage area has not smelled that good since.

Author Kent Whitaker's wife and son are shown in 2008 atop the Hixson Motorsports Hauler during an NASCAR and ARCA race weekend. Later in the day the family visited with several team cooks preparing meals for their teams.

4 pounds pork back ribs (or meaty spareribs)

1 tablespoon brown sugar

1 tablespoon paprika

1 tablespoon onion powder

¾ teaspoon celery salt

½ teaspoon cumin

½ teaspoon pepper

3 cups hickory wood chips

Cut ribs into 4 portions and place in a shallow dish. In a small bowl, combine brown sugar, paprika, onion powder, celery salt, cumin and black pepper; rub evenly over meaty side of ribs. Cover ribs with plastic wrap and marinate in the refrigerator 4 to 24 hours.

At least 1 hour before grilling, soak wood chips in enough water to cover. Drain before using.

In charcoal grill with a cover, place preheated coals around a drip pan for medium indirect heat. Add ½ inch hot water to drip pan. Sprinkle half the drained wood chips over coals.

Place ribs, bone side down, on grill rack over drip pan. Cover and grill 1½ to 2 hours or until ribs are tender. Add more preheated coals (use a hibachi or a metal chimney starter to preheat coals) and wood chips if needed. Turn ribs halfway through grilling.

Recipe Courtesy of the National Pork Board

Serious Grilling

Bourbon and Butter Mopped Baby Back Ribs

Keep this Bourbon and Butter Mop Sauce recipe in your pantry bag of tricks for other cuts of meat.

2 racks baby back pork ribs

BOURBON AND BUTTER MOP SAUCE:

1 stick butter

1½ cups apple cider

¼ cup bourbon

3 tablespoons soy sauce

2 tablespoons orange juice

2 tablespoons water

RIB RUB:

3 tablespoons brown sugar

2 tablespoons sea salt

2 tablespoons paprika or smoked paprika

1 tablespoon black pepper

3 teaspoons dry mustard

2 teaspoons garlic powder

2 teaspoons cumin powder

Place ribs, meat side down, on a cookie sheet or large foil pan. Remove or score membrane on backside of ribs.

Brush mop sauce over ribs and then massage rub evenly into meat. Cover ribs with plastic cling wrap or foil and refrigerate several hours or overnight.

Set up your grill for indirect grilling. Shoot for a temperature of 325° to 350° with drip pan and soaked wood chips. Cook ribs 45 to 60 minutes with grill lid closed. Wait until ribs have cooked about 30 minutes for brushing on additional mop sauce so you won't brush off rub. Mop and turn as needed with grill lid closed as much as possible.

Before serving, place ribs over direct heat and coat with your favorite barbecue sauce. Grill a few more minutes to thicken sauce. Rest ribs several minutes before serving.

For Bourbon and Butter Mop Sauce: Melt butter in a large saucepan over medium-high heat. Add apple cider, bourbon, soy sauce, orange juice and water; mix well.

For Rib Rub: Combine ingredients and mix well.

Raspberry Infused Barbecue Sauced Beef Back Ribs

1 tablespoon garlic powder

1 tablespoon pepper

1 tablespoon salt

1 tablespoon brown sugar

2 slabs beef back ribs

½ cup chopped onion

½ cup ketchup

½ cup raspberry jelly or jam

¼ cup beer

¼ cup whiskey

¼ cup real butter

Combine garlic powder, pepper, salt and brown sugar in a bowl. Rub into ribs. Place ribs in a covered dish or freezer bag and place in the fridge overnight.

Combine remaining ingredients and brush on ribs.

Grill or smoke over medium indirect heat about 4 hours with cover closed. Increase to medium-high heat and grill 6 to 8 minutes while basting. Serve hot.

Serious Grilling

Texas Grilled Beef Back Ribs

Tailgate Friendly

5 pounds beef back ribs

Salt and pepper to taste

Chili powder to taste

Cumin powder to taste

1½ tablespoons vegetable oil

1½ cups finely chopped onion

1 jalapeño, seeded and chopped
(or 1 tablespoon store-bought
chopped jalapeño)

1 tablespoon minced garlic

½ tablespoon cumin powder

1½ teaspoons crushed red
pepper flakes

1½ cups taco or chili sauce

½ cup water

½ cup ketchup

3 tablespoons fresh lemon juice

Cut ribs into 2 to 3 bone sections and sprinkle with salt, pepper, chili powder and cumin to taste. (Don't go overboard on cumin, as it's in the sauce as well.) Set aside while you prepare your grill and sauce.

Heat oil in a saucepan; add onion, jalapeño, garlic, cumin and red pepper flakes. Cook and stir until onion and jalapeños are tender. Add taco or chili sauce, water, ketchup and lemon juice. Bring to a boil then cover and reduce to low, stirring frequently. Season with salt.

Set up covered charcoal or gas grill for indirect cooking with wood chips. Reserve ½ cup sauce in a separate bowl for basting (so you won't contaminate the entire saucepan with raw meat). Evenly brush each rib section with sauce from saucepan. Place ribs in a large foil pan and drizzle with more sauce. Cover tightly with foil and place pan on grill.

Cooked with lid closed for 1½ to 2 hours, rotating pan about every 30 minutes. You can open foil and rearrange ribs if needed.

When ribs are tender, remove from foil pan and place them directly over hotter part of grill about 10 minutes just to brown edges and add grill marks. Baste with reserved sauce before serving.

Wild Boar Barbecue Ribs

While writing for Racing Milestones covering the NASCAR foodie scene, one of the most interesting recipes came from former driver Kerry Earnhardt who is fond of wild boar ribs. Kerry, along with his siblings Kelly and Dale, have taken their love of the outdoors to a new level with Earnhardt Outdoors — a lifestyle brand designed to pass on the traditions and values obtained from their forefathers to the next generation of outdoor enthusiasts.

2 racks wild boar ribs

Liquid smoke

Worcestershire sauce

¾ cup brown sugar

1½ tablespoons paprika

1½ tablespoons garlic powder

2 teaspoons salt

2 teaspoons black pepper

1 teaspoon crushed red pepper

Barbecue sauce

Remove membrane from back of the ribs or heavily score it with a knife. Cut ribs in half, quarters, or single rib portions and sprinkle with liquid smoke and Worcestershire sauce. Allow them to rest in a baking dish or deep sided baking pan lined with aluminum foil.

Combine brown sugar, paprika, garlic powder, salt, black pepper and red pepper. Rub each piece evenly with seasoning. Cover pan tightly with aluminum foil and place in a preheated 300° covered grill. Grill 2 hours with cover closed.

Check ribs every 20 to 30 minutes to rotate or move to another place on the grill to avoid burning. The idea is to steam and cook ribs in tightly sealed foil to keep them moist and make them tender.

Remove ribs from pan and place directly on grill grate while basting with your favorite barbecue sauce. Grill until outside edges turn golden and brown with nice grill marks.

Rest rib 2 to 3 minutes before serving hot.

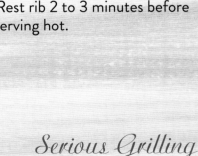

Serious Grilling

Salt and Pepper Lamb Ribs

When people think of ribs they generally think of secret barbecue sauces and rubs bursting with flavor. There's one exception to the rule — lamb ribs. The secret is to not overwhelm the flavor of the lamb.

1 rack lamb ribs, cut to one-bone pieces

2 tablespoons olive oil

½ lime or lemon, juiced

Salt and pepper to taste

Parsley for garnish

Place lamb ribs in a glass baking dish and brush with olive oil. Drizzle with lime or lemon juice and sprinkle salt and pepper. Allow seasonings to soak into meat while you prepare the grill.

Grill lamb ribs over medium-high heat, turning, until golden brown with grill marks, 8 to 12 minutes per side or to an internal temperature of 145°. Top with parsley before serving.

Kiss of the Mediterranean Lamb Ribs

Lamb ribs, cut to one-bone pieces

Salt and pepper to taste

1 (6-ounce) carton plain yogurt

1 tablespoon olive oil

½ lime or lemon, juiced

Dash allspice

Parsley

Dash mint

Dash cinnamon

Place lamb ribs in a glass baking dish and sprinkle with a light amount of salt and pepper.

Combine yogurt and remaining ingredients in a bowl and mix well. Brush over ribs. Cover and chill at least an hour and while preparing grill.

Grill lamb ribs over medium-high heat, turning, until golden brown with grill marks to an internal temperature of 145°.

STEAKS BY FIRE

BEST STEAKS FOR GRILLING:

Ribeye steak, Top Loin steak, T-Bone steak, Top Sirloin steak, Tenderloin, Top Blade steak.

APPROPRIATE CUTS IF MARINATED:

Flank steak, Shoulder steak, Blade steak (7-bone steak), and Skirt steak.

WHAT DOES "I WANT MY STEAK RARE" ACTUALLY MEAN?

Steak doneness is determined by the internal temperature of the steak. Remove steaks from heat when about 5 degrees lower than desired doneness, as the steaks will continue to cook a bit while resting.

DONENESS CHART:

Very Rare ....130°
Rare.......................140°
Medium Rare..........145°
Medium...................160°
Well Done ....170°
Very Well Done ......180°

Serious Grilling

Grilling Times for Steaks

Not sure how long to cook your steak? Let's ask the pros. The Texas Beef Council suggests this chart to best plan your grilling time for steaks. Keep in mind that times will vary between grills, outside temps, etc.

BEEF CUTS	THICKNESS / WEIGHT	TOTAL COOKING TIME
Top Round	¾ in.	8 to 9 minutes
	1 in.	16 to 18 minutes
	1½ in.	25 to 28 minutes (covered)
Chuck Shoulder	¾ in.	14 to 17 minutes
	1 in.	16 to 20 minutes
Chuck Blade	¾ to 1 in.	15 to 18 minutes
Flank	1½ to 2 lbs.	17 to 21 minutes
Skirt	1 to 1½ lbs.	6 to 8 minutes
Tenderloin	1 in.	13 to 15 minutes
Ribeye, Boneless	¾ in.	6 to 8 minutes
	1 in.	11 to 14 minutes
Ribeye, Bone-In	¾ in.	6 to 8 minutes
	1 in.	9 to 12 minutes
T-Bone/Porterhouse	¾ in.	10 to 12 minutes
	1 in.	14 to 16 minutes
Top Loin (Strip)	¾ in.	10 to 12 minute
	1 in.	14 to 16 minutes
Top Sirloin	¾ in.	13 to 16 minutes
	1 in.	17 to 21 minutes
Sirloin Kabobs	1 to 1½ in. cubes	5 to 7 minutes
	2 in. cubes	8 to 10 minutes
Top Blade	¾ in.	8 minutes

SUPER SIMPLE STEAK RECIPES

Choose a tender cut of steak such as ribeye, chuck eye, T-bone or New York Strip. Just season and grill to perfection. Get ready, these cook up super fast!

Pineapple Steaks

4 tender steaks such as ribeyes

1 (15-ounce) can sliced pineapple, reserve juice

½ cup soy sauce

Dash ginger

2 tablespoons brown sugar

Salt and pepper to taste

Marinate steaks in a glass baking dish using pineapple juice, soy sauce, ginger and brown sugar. Cover and chill to 3 hours. Grill steaks to your liking with pineapple slices to the side. Allow steaks to rest a few minutes before serving. Sprinkle with salt and pepper; serve topped with grilled pineapple slices.

Salsa Topped Fiesta Steaks

4 steaks of your choice

1 (12-ounce) can beer

2 tablespoons allspice

2 tablespoons lime juice

Cumin powder to taste

Garlic salt to taste

Your favorite salsa

Use a meat hammer to pound steaks then marinate in a glass baking dish using beer, all-spice, lime juice, cumin and garlic salt. Marinate 2 hours for tender cuts (up to overnight for tougher cuts). Grill steaks to your liking over medium heat. Allow steaks to rest a few minutes before serving. Top steaks with your favorite salsa.

Horseradish Kissed Ribeye Steaks

4 ribeye steaks

Salt and pepper to taste

3 to 4 tablespoons plain yogurt

2 tablespoons steak sauce

1 tablespoon prepared horseradish

Rub steaks with salt and pepper and place in glass baking dish. Combine yogurt, steak sauce and horseradish in a bowl and mix. Brush steaks with marinade, cover and chill before grilling. Grill steaks to your liking and allow them to rest for a few minutes before serving.

Chuck Eye Steaks with Rosemary Thyme Flavored Butter

4 chuck eye steaks (or ribeye steaks)

Olive oil

Salt and pepper to taste

4 to 5 tablespoons butter

1 tablespoon finely chopped rosemary

1 teaspoon thyme

1 teaspoon garlic powder

Brush steaks with olive oil and rub with salt and pepper. Soften butter in a bowl and add rosemary, thyme and garlic powder. Return butter to fridge to chill and set.

Grill steaks to your liking and allow them to rest a few minutes before serving. Top with rosemary thyme butter.

Wine-Basted Ribeye Steaks with Simple Hollandaise Sauce

2 to 4 ribeye steaks

Salt, pepper and garlic powder to taste

⅓ cup red wine

⅓ cup steak sauce

HOLLANDAISE SAUCE:

8 ounces (2 sticks) butter

3 large egg yolks

1 tablespoon lemon juice

Dash salt and pepper

2 tablespoons hot water

Parsley flakes, optional

Gently rub steaks with salt, pepper and garlic powder. Place on a plate and refrigerate 5 to 30 minutes.

Combine red wine and steak sauce in a small bowl to use as a baste.

Grill steaks over medium-high heat, basting occasionally and turning as few times as possible. Allow steaks to rest about 5 minutes before serving with warm Hollandaise Sauce drizzled on top.

For Sauce: Melt butter in a small saucepan over medium heat. Remove pan from heat when butter is completely melted.

In a bowl, whisk together egg yolks, lemon juice, salt and pepper. Add melted butter and water; whisk 2 minutes.

Return entire mixture to saucepan over low heat and whisk constantly until slightly thickened. Remove from heat. Add parsley flakes for a touch of color, if desired. Serve over steaks.

Serious Grilling

Super Simple Salt and Pepper Ribeyes

My buddy Rusty Eager in Texas says, "I do these quickly making them perfect for the back yard, the campground or kitchen."

4 ribeye steaks, 1 inch thick

½ cup Dale's marinade

Coarse salt to taste

Fresh cracked pepper to taste

Marinate steaks in Dale's marinade a few minutes. Remove from marinade and rub salt and pepper into steaks. (Don't just sprinkle; rub.) Grill over high heat (or cook in skillet) to your liking. Before serving, allow steaks to rest a few minutes and sprinkle lightly with more cracked black pepper.

Easy Pabst Blue Ribbon Chuck Eye Steaks

4 to 6 chuck eye steaks

1 (12-ounce) Pabst Blue Ribbon beer

1 tablespoon steak sauce

2 tablespoons minced garlic

2 tablespoons lemon pepper seasoning

Paprika to taste

Cumin powder to taste

Salt and pepper to taste

1 package béarnaise sauce mix

Marinate steaks in a glass baking dish with PBR and steak sauce. Cover and chill 2 to 3 hours (or longer).

Remove steaks from marinade and rub lightly with minced garlic, lemon pepper, paprika, cumin, salt and pepper.

Prepare béarnaise sauce as directed on package.

Grill steaks (or pan-sear steaks with olive oil) to desired temperature, turning as few times as possible. Serve topped with béarnaise sauce (mixed according to package directions).

Honey Mustard Grilled Beef Medallions

4 beef medallion steaks, 1 inch thick

Salt and pepper to taste

⅓ cup honey

⅓ cup Dijon mustard

1 tablespoon lime juice

½ tablespoon cumin powder

2 teaspoons soy sauce

Dash sugar

Place steaks in a glass dish and rub with salt and pepper. Combine remaining ingredients in a bowl and coat steaks. Cover and chill at least 1 hour. (I like to prep these around lunch time in order to grill for an evening meal.)

Grill over high heat turning only once or twice. Since you're grilling over high heat your total grilling time would be about 6 minutes (3 minutes each side), depending on your grill and steak thickness, which will give you a nice seared outside with a tender pinkish middle.

Remove from heat, rest a few minutes and serve hot.

Montreal Steak Seasoned Filet Mignon

4 filet mignon cuts, about 1½ inches thick

Vegetable or canola oil

2 tablespoons paprika

2 tablespoons crushed black pepper

2 tablespoons kosher salt

1 tablespoon granulated garlic

1 tablespoon granulated onion

1 tablespoon crushed coriander

1 tablespoon dill

1 tablespoon crushed red pepper flakes

Brush steaks with oil. Mix remaining ingredients in a bowl and rub over each steak. Grill steaks over medium-high heat to your desired temperature.

Serious Grilling

Marinated Dijon Mustard T-Bone Steaks

I prefer this recipe with T-Bones and Porterhouse steaks.

2 T-Bone steaks

⅓ cup Dijon mustard

1 tablespoon lemon juice

1 tablespoon minced garlic

½ teaspoon salt

½ teaspoon pepper

Dash thyme

Place steaks in a glass dish. Combine remaining ingredients in a bowl to make a marinade. Pour over steaks, cover and chill in fridge 2 hours or longer before cooking. (I prefer overnight if possible.)

Grill over medium-high high heat to your desired temperature.

WHO INVENTED KETCHUP AND MUSTARD PACKETS?

Have you been through a drive through or dined at a fast food restaurant and asked for extra ketchup or mustard? Those little squeeze packs of our favorite condiments are a relatively new invention coming a decade after World War Two. In 1955 Harold Ross and Yale Kaplan received a patent for "Dispensing containers for liquids." Their design is relatively unchanged today.

Vegetable Stuffed Rolled Steak

1 shank, flank or skirt steak
(largest and thinnest cut you
can find)

¼ cup olive oil

Salt and pepper to taste

4 ounces flavored whipped
cream cheese spread

2 carrots, thin-sliced
lengthwise

1 sweet onion, thin-sliced

1 cup spinach leaves

1 small squash, thin-sliced
lengthwise

1 tablespoon garlic powder

1 teaspoon thyme

1 tablespoon parsley

3 slices provolone cheese

½ cup steak sauce

Pound steak with hammer-style tenderizer to ¼ inch thick. Lay steak out on a cookie sheet; brush with olive oil and sprinkle with salt and pepper.

Spread cream cheese over steak. Top with vegetables and remaining spices, parsley, and cheese. Gently roll steak and secure with cooking string or toothpicks. Baste with steak sauce and grill over high heat to brown edges.

Wrap in foil and continue to cook about 20 more minutes on an upper rack. Turn and rotate often. Remove, unwrap and slice carefully.

Serious Grilling

Red Wine Marinated Grilled Flank Steaks

The secret to grilling a tender flank steak is to marinate the steak overnight and do not overgrill – aim for a medium temperature.

1 (1½- to 2-pound) beef flank steak

½ cup dry red wine

⅓ cup finely chopped onion

1½ tablespoons brown sugar

2 tablespoons lime juice

2 tablespoons soy sauce

1½ tablespoons vegetable oil

2 teaspoons minced garlic

Salt and pepper to taste

Place steak in a glass baking dish (or heavy-duty zip-close bag). Combine remaining ingredients in small bowl and mix well. Pour marinade over steaks, making sure they are evenly coated. Cover dish (or close bag) and marinate in refrigerator at least 6 hours or overnight. Turn steaks a few times during marinating process.

Remove steak from marinade (reserve marinade) and place on a preheated grill over medium-high heat. Pour reserved marinade in a saucepan and bring to a quick boil. Use this mixture to baste steak while grilling.

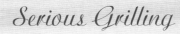

Serious Grilling

Dark Beer Grilled Flank Steaks with Grilled Peppers and Onions

This recipe really makes a flank steak a great grilling choice. The best results come with marinating the steaks overnight.

2 large flank steaks

Extra virgin olive oil

1 (12-ounce) bottle dark beer

½ cup Worcestershire sauce

1½ tablespoons Italian seasoning

½ tablespoon ground cumin

Coarse salt to taste

Cracked black pepper to taste

1 red bell pepper, sliced

1 yellow bell pepper, sliced

2 small onions, sliced

Place steaks on a cutting board and lightly score in a criss-cross pattern with a sharp knife. Don't cut into meat too deeply, no more than ⅛ inch deep.

Place steaks in a glass baking dish and brush lightly with olive oil. Set aside 5 to 10 minutes for olive oil to soak into score marks. Pour beer and Worcestershire over steaks. Turn to coat evenly, remove and rub Italian seasoning, cumin, salt and pepper into steaks. (Double dry ingredients if needed, depending on size of steaks.)

Return to marinade and turn to coat. Add bell peppers and onions and stir to get them covered with some of the liquid. Cover and chill overnight (or at least 2 to 3 hours), turning occasionally.

Grill steaks over medium-high heat to desired temperature, 4 to 5 minutes per side should be medium-rare.

Grill onions and peppers as well, using a grill basket. When done, remove steaks from heat and rest 5 minutes before cutting. Slice against the grain into thin pieces for tender results. Serve topped with grilled peppers and onions.

Petite Sirloin with Port Mushroom Shallot Sauce

This sauce requires a little prep work but is well worth the effort. I suggest starting the sauce about an hour before you plan on grilling.

4 petite sirloin steaks

Salt and pepper to taste

PORT MUSHROOM SHALLOT SAUCE:

5 to 6 shallots, peeled and cut

½ cup sliced mushrooms

3½ teaspoons olive oil

1 teaspoon minced garlic

4½ cups ruby port wine

4 tablespoons butter

Salt and pepper to taste

Rub steaks with salt and pepper and set aside as your grill readies. Grill over medium-high heat to desired temperature. Baste with Port Mushroom Shallot Sauce, if desired. Serve steaks drizzled with Port Mushroom Shallot Sauce.

For Sauce: Preheat oven to broil. In a bowl, coat shallots and mushrooms with olive oil and garlic. Place on a cookie sheet and broil until slightly soft and edges begin to brown. Remove from the oven and finely chop (or use a food processor).

Place wine in a saucepan over medium-high heat and cook about 30 minutes to reduce. Add butter, shallots and mushrooms mix; season to taste with salt and pepper. Reduce heat to low and cook, covered, as you grill the steaks.

IKE LIKED GRILLING

President Dwight David "Ike" Eisenhower considered himself to be quite the grilling expert. He loved to cook outdoors and his favorite meal was steaks grilled over charcoal.

Serious Grilling

Orange Rubbed Top Sirloin Steaks with Creamy Orange Steak Sauce

1 tablespoon orange zest

½ tablespoon minced garlic

1½ teaspoons salt

1½ teaspoons pepper

2 to 4 top sirloin steaks, up to 1 inch thick

Oil

CREAMY ORANGE STEAK SAUCE:

2½ tablespoons freshly squeezed orange juice

½ cup plain yogurt or plain Greek yogurt

½ cup steak sauce

½ tablespoon dried cilantro

1 teaspoon chipotle powder

Salt to taste

Combine zest, garlic, salt and pepper in a small bowl. Lightly brush each steak with a bit of oil and rub with orange zest mixture.

Grill steaks over medium-high heat to desired temperature.

For Sauce: While steaks are on the grill, combine orange juice, yogurt, steak sauce, cilantro, chipotle powder, and salt in medium bowl. Serve steaks with a side of sauce.

Tennessee Whiskey & Cola Glazed New York Strips

Whiskey or bourbon both work great – it's your choice. I prefer a New York strip or ribeye for this dish, but you can use less tender cuts if you increase the marinade time.

4 New York strips (or ribeye steaks)

½ cup Tennessee whiskey or bourbon

½ cup cola (not diet)

¼ cup brown sugar

¼ cup soy sauce

2 tablespoons lemon juice

1 tablespoon minced garlic

Salt and pepper to taste

Place steaks in a glass baking dish (or heavy-duty zip-close bag). Combine remaining ingredients in a bowl. Cover steaks with marinade and cover bowl (or seal bag) and chill 2 to 3 hours. Grill steaks to desired temperature over medium-high heat.

Before you grill steaks, start Finishing Glaze. Combine all ingredients and boil in a saucepan until reduced by half. Drizzle over steaks before serving.

FINISHING GLAZE:

½ cup Tennessee whiskey or bourbon

1 cup cola (not diet)

¼ cup brown sugar

¼ cup soy sauce

2 tablespoons lemon juice

1 tablespoon minced garlic

Salt and pepper to taste

2 tablespoons minced onion, optional

2 tablespoons minced jalapeño, optional

Serious Grilling

Hot Coffee New York Strip

1 pound New York strip steak

1 tablespoon olive oil

HOT COFFEE RUB:

1 tablespoon brown sugar

1 tablespoon salt

½ tablespoon black pepper

½ tablespoon red pepper flakes

½ tablespoon coffee grounds

½ tablespoon garlic powder

½ tablespoon smoked paprika

Rub steak with olive oil.

Combine Hot Coffee Rub ingredients and mix well. Rub generously over steak. Set aside at about 1 hour to come to room temperature.

Heat coals on one side of grill to medium-hot. Sear steak 2 minutes on each side over coals. Move to cool side of grill, close lid and 20 minutes or to desired temperature. Rest steak 10 minutes before serving.

Grilled Sirloin Tip Steaks with Wet Ancho Chili Lime Rub

2 beef sirloin tip center steaks

1½ tablespoons oil

1 tablespoon lime juice

2 tablespoons ancho chili powder

1½ tablespoons minced garlic

1 tablespoon onion powder

2½ teaspoons dried oregano (or Italian seasoning)

2 teaspoons unsweetened cocoa powder

½ teaspoon ground cinnamon

Place steaks in a glass baking dish. For wet rub, combine remaining ingredients in a small bowl and mix well to form of a paste. Evenly coat steaks with rub, cover and chill 2 to 3 hours.

Grill over medium-high heat, turning as few times as possible, to your desired temperature.

Serious Grilling

Kent's St. Louis Beef Tips and Cream Sauce

Ally and I had the opportunity to do a series of chef demos in St. Louis in association with the Balloon Festival. We had a great time visiting different parts of the city, parks and the Arch. We even stayed in a hotel that was supposedly haunted. And, according to our dog Moses, it probably was. That's another story! Here's the recipe I used during the demos and for the local news stations and outlets.

1 pound beef stew meat or cubed chuck eye steak

⅔ cup steak marinade (or steak sauce)

⅔ cup orange juice

CREAM SAUCE:

1 cup sour cream

1 cup mayonnaise

2 tablespoons milk

½ (1.25-ouce) packet spaghetti sauce mix

Parsley or minced garlic, optional

Place steaks, marinade and orange juice in a plastic zip-close bag and chill overnight (or at least 3 hours).

Remove steaks and boil marinade to use as a baste. Grill beef tips, basting occasionally, to desired temperature.

Serve over seasoned and steamed vegetables, rice or noodles drizzled with Cream Sauce.

For Cream Sauce: Combine everything in a small bowl, cover, and chill before serving.

The great thing about this simple recipe is that almost everyone already has the ingredients in their kitchen. The trick is to marinate the meat overnight if possible, or at least for a few hours.

TASTES LIKE CHICKEN

One of the easiest meats to grill is chicken. And yet, one of the hardest meats to cook on a grill is also chicken. Why? Because chicken has two distinct types of meat – dark and white.

DARKER MEATS grill perfectly due to a higher fat content. It's hard to mess up grilled wings, drumsticks or thighs. Just season your dark meat cuts, and grill until they are fully cooked.

WHITE MEAT, such as chicken breast, is leaner and will dry out if overcooked. A drip pan with water and a bit of beer or juice will add moisture during cooking. A brine works well also.

BRINING CHICKEN: A simple low-salt brine helps to keep poultry moist while cooking. Cover your chicken with cold water; add a few dashes of salt and a few tablespoons of apple juice. Cover and refrigerate overnight. Discard brine before grilling.

SAFE CHICKEN IS GOOD CHICKEN: Always thaw chicken in the fridge and never on a counter. Be mindful of splashes and drips when handling raw meat. Be sure to clean up, wipe up and wash your hands frequently, and always just after finishing raw chicken prep. Think of cross contamination this way: would you put the towels you used to dry your dog off after a bath back in the closet with fresh clean towels? Nope!

All poultry – whether it's the whole bird, breasts, legs, thighs, wings, ground poultry, and even stuffing should be cooked to an internal temperature of 165°.

Using rubs that have a high salt content can cause poultry to dry out. So, choose rubs that are not salt heavy.

Serious Grilling

Chili Lime Chicken with Southwestern Bean and Corn Relish

The recipe lends itself to boneless chicken breasts and tenders that can be topped with the corn relish (but don't shy away from other cuts). Another option is boneless, skinless breasts pounded thin then stuffed with the salsa. There are plenty of combinations. I suggest getting the relish going first so you can chill it for a while to really boost the flavors.

GRILLED CHILI LIME CHICKEN:

3 to 4 chicken breasts

1 lime, juiced

Hot sauce to taste

3 tablespoons chili powder

2 tablespoons paprika, smoked if desired

1 tablespoon cumin powder

Cilantro to taste, optional

BEAN AND CORN RELISH:

1 (15-ounce) can whole-kernel corn, drained

1 (15-ounce) can black beans, drained and rinsed

1 (10-ounce) can Rotel tomatoes

½ cup chopped red onion

½ cup chopped sweet onion

2 to 3 tablespoons chopped fresh cilantro

3 tablespoons lime juice

2 tablespoons chopped jalapeño

½ tablespoon cumin powder

1 tablespoon vegetable oil

1 clove garlic, minced

Place chicken in a glass bowl, drizzle with lime juice and top with hot sauce to taste. Rest chicken 5 to 15 minutes. In a bowl, combine chili powder, paprika, cumin and cilantro; rub over chicken.

Grill chicken over medium-high heat until done, turning as needed. Serve hot with relish on the side (or on top).

For Relish: Combine all ingredients in a bowl and mix well. Cover and chill.

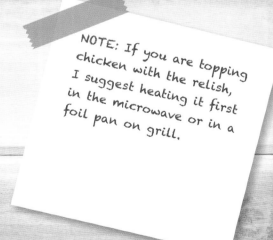

NOTE: If you are topping chicken with the relish, I suggest heating it first in the microwave or in a foil pan on grill.

Citrus Beer Can Chicken

I have enjoyed many beer can chicken recipes over the years. The simple version is to stick a large whole chicken on an opened beer can, balance it on the grate of your heated grill, and close the lid. Once you have those easy steps down, you've opened the door to countless variations. It's important to use a covered grill.

1 large whole chicken

1 orange, juiced, divided

1 lemon, juiced

2 tablespoons allspice, divided

1 (12-ounce) can beer

½ tablespoon garlic powder

Rinse chicken and pat dry.

Reserve 1 tablespoon orange juice. Rub chicken inside and out with remaining orange juice and lemon juice.

Sprinkle 1 tablespoon allspice inside chicken and remaining 1 tablespoon outside. Pour half the beer into a glass and reserve. Poke a few additional holes in the top of the can.

Add reserved orange juice and garlic powder to beer can, then pour about half the beer in the glass back on into the can. Carefully place can inside chicken (chicken will be sitting upright on can) and use it and the legs to balance chicken on a small foil pan on your grill grate. (You can buy a holder to help balance the chicken or use pieces of foil to help firm things up.)

Grill using indirect heat or directly over medium-high heat with lid closed. Grill until skin is deep brown and internal temp is 165°.

4 Variations on Beer Can Chicken

Here are a couple of easy twists to the traditional beer can chicken recipe. Cooking chicken on a can is a great idea because the liquid heats up, steams and adds moisture and flavor to the bird...from the inside. You'll still want to season the outside of your bird as well. Use butter or oil with a seasoning mix or rub. There's always some extra room in the cavity of the bird for flavor boosters such as onion slices, bell pepper, hot peppers, pineapple, orange slices, lemon, lime and more.

SERIOUS BEER LOVERS BEER CAN CHICKEN:

I have some friends who are serious about their beer drinking. Not as in overdoing it...but they go about it like they were at a fine wine tasting, matching their beer to a menu like one would do with wine. So, why not use something other than a run of the mill can of beer? Try using your favorite local craft beer or a seasonal beer from your favorite brewer. Darker beers will offer up a deeper flavor.

SODA CAN CHICKEN

Hey, other beverages come in a can, Why not choose something like a can of root beer, orange soda, or cola? Try combining orange soda with ginger ale and a splash of lemon or lime juice. A can of root beer with some minced onion is another way to go.

JUICED UP CHICKEN!

Instead of beer or soda, try using juice...orange juice, pineapple juice or any fruit juice you enjoy. Save an empty beer or soda can, rinse it out, and fill it with your chosen juice and a few favorite spices.

TEXAS DANCING CHICKEN

My buddy George from Texas cooks Beer Can Chicken Tex-Mex Style by adding chili powder and cumin to the beer. George says he knows his chickens are done when the skin is golden brown and drawn tight causing the wings to rise up. "It looks like they're dancing."

Crunchy Zesty Italian Chicken Breasts

4 to 6 boneless skinless
  chicken breasts

1 (16-ounce) bottle robust or
  zesty Italian dressing, divided

1 cup crushed croutons

½ cup freshly shredded
  Parmesan cheese (not the
  shaker kind because you
  want the cheese to melt)

½ cup shredded
  mozzarella cheese

Place chicken in a covered bowl (or zip-close bag); top with dressing, reserving some for basting. Cover bowl (or close bag) and chill several hours (or overnight) before grilling.

Grill chicken over medium-high heat, turning as needed. Baste with additional dressing as chicken cooks.

Before removing chicken from grill, sprinkle with crushed croutons followed by cheese. Sprinkle more croutons over cheese. When cheese melts, serve chicken hot with your choice of sides or over a salad.

TIP: Flatten chicken by placing between two pieces of cling wrap and pound using a meat tenderizing hammer. The thinner pieces are perfect for holding the melted cheese and crumbled croutons in place.

Serious Grilling

Kent's Nearly Famous Root Beer Chicken

Several years ago, a newspaper ran a story about me featuring a picture of me by a grill with a caption that read something like "Kent grilling his favorite Root Beer Chicken." People called for weeks wanting to know what it was and how to make it. The idea for the recipe was not actually mine. While watching a documentary, the narrator mentioned Elvis, Vegas and Root Beer Chicken. So I came up with my own recipe. I spent many nights emailing food lovers this simple recipe. I actually got an email back from one nice lady who accused me of leaving out a secret ingredient because it seemed too easy.

6 to 8 chicken leg quarters

1 (2-liter) bottle root beer

5 garlic cloves, minced

1 small onion, chopped

Salt and pepper to taste

1 tablespoon brown sugar

SLICED POTATOES:

3 to 4 potatoes

Olive oil

Cajun seasoning

Place chicken quarters in a large pan or bowl. Pour root beer over chicken to cover (it may not require the entire bottle). Add garlic and onion; cover with cling wrap. Refrigerate overnight.

Next day, remove chicken from marinade; reserve marinade. Place chicken on smoker (or use a grill and indirect heat).

As chicken smokes, pour root beer marinade in a saucepan over medium-high heat. Add a dash of salt and pepper and 1 tablespoon brown sugar. Boil it down for about 30 minutes and use as a basting sauce on chicken.

For Potatoes: Peel potatoes and slice into ⅛- to ¼-inch thick chip-like slices. Coat lightly with olive oil and Cajun seasoning to taste.

Oil cooking grate and grill until golden, turning as needed.

Tastes Like Chicken

Simmering Heat Peach Glazed Chicken

Choose your cut of chicken and get started. This recipe is perfect for everything from breasts and tenders to thighs and wings.

2 chicken breast

1 cup peach preserves

2 tablespoons cider vinegar

1 tablespoon hot sauce

2 teaspoons ground ginger

2 teaspoons ancho chili powder

Rinse chicken well, and set aside. Combine remaining ingredients in a small saucepan and heat just until well mixed.

Grill chicken over medium-high heat turning as needed until they start to turn golden. Baste chicken with sauce as it finishes cooking.

Simple Grilled Jerk Chicken

2 chicken breasts, cut into 4 strips each (or 8 large chicken tenders)

2 tablespoons crushed red pepper, divided

1 tablespoon brown sugar

1 tablespoon allspice

½ cup vinegar

½ cup pineapple juice (or orange juice)

½ onion, chopped, divided

Rinse chicken well and set aside.

In a large bowl, combine 1 tablespoon red pepper, brown sugar, allspice, vinegar, juice, and half the onion. Mix well and then add chicken. Cover, or use a zip-close bag, and marinate 2 to 3 hours in refrigerator.

Grill chicken over medium-high heat, turning as needed. Before removing from grill sprinkle with remaining chopped onion and red pepper flakes. Serve hot.

Serious Grilling

Lemon Balsamic Chicken Breasts

4 chicken breasts, boneless and skinless

1 tablespoon olive oil

½ teaspoon balsamic vinegar

1 lemon, juiced

Lemon pepper to taste

1 cup shredded Italian blend cheese (or Parmesan cheese)

BALSAMIC MUSTARD SAUCE:

1 cup dark brown sugar

½ cup Dijon mustard

½ cup balsamic vinegar

¼ cup yellow mustard

¼ teaspoon ground cloves

Place chicken in a glass baking dish. Combine olive oil, balsamic vinegar and lemon juice; rub over chicken. Coat each breast with lemon pepper seasoning.

Cover and chill while preparing grill. You can also go ahead and prepare the sauce as well.

Grill chicken breasts over medium-high heat, turning as needed, to an internal temperature of 165°. Before removing chicken from grill, brush with Balsamic Mustard Sauce. Turn and coat evenly.

Top with a small amount of cheese before serving.

For Sauce: Combine all ingredients in a small saucepan over low heat. Simmer 8 to 10 minutes, allowing the sauce to thicken. Remove pan from heat and set aside.

Fajita Chicken with White Jalapeño Cheese Sauce

4 to 6 boneless skinless chicken breasts

½ lemon, juiced

1 (1.25-ounce) packet fajita seasoning

White Jalapeño Cheese Sauce

WHITE JALAPEÑO CHEESE SAUCE:

1 tablespoon butter

3 tablespoons minced onion

1 tablespoon minced jalapeño

½ pound white American cheese, cubed

2 tablespoons milk

1 tablespoon sour cream, optional

Place chicken in a glass baking dish and top with lemon juice. Gently rub each breast with fajita seasoning. Cover and chill 30 minutes to an hour.

Grill chicken over medium-high heat, turning as needed, until done.

Serve over grilled vegetables or seasoned rice and drizzle with White Jalapeño Cheese Sauce.

For Sauce: Place butter in a saucepan over medium heat. Add onion and jalapeño and sauté until soft (do not brown).

Add cheese, milk and sour cream. Stir until cheese is melted and well mixed. Add additional milk, if needed, to thin.

Serious Grilling

Bacon-Wrapped Grilled Chicken Tenders with Pineapple Dipping Sauce

8 to 10 chicken tenders

2 tablespoons olive oil

4 tablespoons chicken seasoning or rub

8 to 10 bacon slices

Salt and pepper to taste

Brown sugar to taste

PINEAPPLE DIPPING SAUCE:

1 (20-ounce) can crushed pineapple with juice

3 to 4 tablespoons butter

½ cup brown sugar

¼ cup barbecue sauce

2 to 3 teaspoons chili powder

Salt and pepper to taste

1 tablespoon cornstarch, optional

Place chicken tenders in a glass baking dish; brush lightly with olive oil and sprinkle with your favorite chicken seasoning or rub.

Wrap each tender with bacon and secure with a toothpick. Cover and chill for an hour to allow chicken to soak up seasoning.

Prepare grill using a grilling tray, griddle or foil pan; use nonstick spray to prepare the surface. Sprinkle with salt, pepper and a little brown sugar as you grill.

For Sauce: I like to prepare sauce while chicken is chilling. Place pineapple and juice in a blender and pulse a few times to break up pineapple. Add to a saucepan with remaining ingredients, except cornstarch, over medium heat. Cook just until butter is melted and everything is heated through and mixed well. Add cornstarch, if desired, to thicken.

Use as a dipping sauce or drizzle over the top of your chicken.

Sweet Maple & Mustard Grilled Brined Chicken Breasts

If you don't have chicken on hand, this also works well with boneless pork chops. I like to start this well in advance of grilling time. I brine the chicken and make the basting sauce in the morning then do some chores, mow grass, get some work done, nap, etc. Around lunch, I'll switch the chicken from the brine to the marinade then nap, get some chores done, work, or nap...you get the idea. Then, around grilling time that evening I have some incredibly moist, plump and marinated chicken ready to go.

½ tablespoon salt

4 to 6 boneless skinless chicken breasts

SWEET MAPLE & MUSTARD SAUCE:

½ cup maple pancake syrup

½ cup Dijon mustard

1½ tablespoons red wine vinegar

1 tablespoon vegetable oil

½ tablespoon minced garlic

Dash Cajun or Creole seasoning

Parsley flakes

Put a small amount of cold water in a large bowl, add salt and stir until salt has dissolved. Add some additional water (but not so much to overflow when chicken is added); stir. Add chicken breasts and top with additional cold water to cover. Cover and chill 2 hours or longer. Drain brine from bowl.

Pour half of the Sweet Maple & Mustard Sauce over chicken, turning to ensure chicken is completely coated. Cover and chill until grill is ready.

Grill over medium high-heat, turning as needed and basting with remaining sauce.

For Sauce: Combine all ingredients in a bowl, stir, cover and chill.

Southern Buttermilk Marinated "Cut Up" Chickens

2 cups buttermilk

4 teaspoons ginger powder

4 teaspoons garlic powder

4 teaspoons chili powder

2 teaspoons cumin powder

Salt and pepper to taste

1 tablespoon apple cider vinegar

2 chickens, halved or cut-up

Barbecue seasoning (or chicken seasoning), to taste

Combine buttermilk, ginger powder, garlic powder, chili powder, cumin powder, salt, pepper and apple cider vinegar in a large deep bowl. Stir to mix and add chicken. Cover and chill several hours or overnight.

Remove chicken from marinade and season additionally with barbecue seasoning or chicken seasoning.

Grill chicken over medium-high heat, turning as needed, until cooked through and juices run clear to an internal temperature of 165°.

Serious Grilling

Kid-Friendly Italian-Stuffed Chicken

Both versions of these recipes are kid friendly and perfect for young chefs to prepare while an adult does the grilling.

STRING CHEESE VERSION:

4 boneless skinless chicken breasts

1 cup pizza sauce, divided

Italian seasoning to taste

1 to 2 cups baby spinach (no stems)

4 individually wrapped string cheese packs

Several water-soaked toothpicks

Olive oil

First, an adult should butterfly chicken breasts and lay flat, or use a meat pounder to flatten them.

Place ¼ cup pizza sauce in a small bowl and allow the kid to brush chicken with olive oil, then pizza sauce and top with Italian seasoning. (Discard the pizza sauce used for brushing.)

Lay several spinach leaves and a string cheese stick in center of chicken. Carefully fold chicken together like a taco and secure with toothpicks. Brush olive oil on outside and sprinkle with more Italian seasoning.

Grill until chicken is done with golden edges. Remove toothpicks and serve hot with remaining pizza sauce for dipping.

PEPPERONI-STUFFED VERSION:

Mozzarella cheese

4 to 5 slices pepperoni per chicken breast

Follow directions for String Cheese Version, but instead of using string cheese and spinach, substitute mozzarella cheese and pepperoni before folding.

ADULT VERSION:

Mozzarella cheese

4 to 5 slices pepperoni per chicken breast

Other toppings of choice: sliced or chopped roasted tomatoes, mushrooms, olives, onion or peppers

Follow directions for String Cheese Version, but instead of using string cheese, substitute mozzarella cheese and add pepperoni and other toppings of choice to spinach before folding.

Tastes Like Chicken

Hickory-Smoked Chicken Salad

I prefer white meat for this recipe, but use what you have — it's all good.

6 chicken breasts, hickory smoked

1 medium onion, diced

4 stalks celery, diced

¼ cup Dijon mustard

⅔ cup mayonnaise

1 tablespoon basil

1 tablespoon minced garlic

1 tablespoon black pepper

⅓ cup sliced almonds

Grill or smoke chicken breasts as you normally would using hickory chips; cool completely. (Remove skin and debone, if needed.)

Cube chicken and place in a large bowl. Top with remaining ingredients and mix well. Chill before serving.

Pineapple Shredded Chicken Salad

4 to 6 boneless chicken breasts

1 (8-ounce) can crushed pineapple

Salt and pepper to taste

½ cup chopped walnuts

1 cup halved seedless green grapes

1 cup mayonnaise

½ cup sour cream

2 teaspoons paprika

1½ teaspoons celery salt

Place chicken in a covered dish or zip-close bag. Drain pineapple, reserving juice; store pineapple in refrigerator. Pour juice over chicken and marinate in refrigerator, preferably overnight.

Season chicken with salt and pepper and grill over medium-high heat until done.

While chicken grills, place pineapple on a sheet of foil coated with nonstick spray. Grill until light golden edges appear.

Cool chicken and pineapple completely. Shred chicken into large pieces with a fork.

Combine chicken and pineapple with remaining ingredients; cover and chill before serving.

Rocket City Hot Grilled Chicken

Because this recipe is "hot as a rocket," I dedicate it to Linda and Sonny (a.k.a. Homer Hickman, author of The Rocket Boys, which was made into the movie October Sky starring Jake Gyllenhaal). They have meant a bunch to my son and our family over the years.

4 to 6 skinless chicken breasts or
   10 to 12 large chicken tenders

1 (4-ouce) can green chiles

¼ cup chopped jalapeños

½ cup minced onion

¼ cup minced carrot

¼ cup minced celery

¼ cup minced green bell pepper

1 tablespoon olive oil

Allspice, salt and pepper to taste

1 (8-ounce) can sliced pineapple

Combine everything, except pineapple slices, in a large covered dish. Marinate 2 hours or longer.

Place chicken on grill. Bring marinade to a quick boil and use it to baste chicken.

When chicken is almost done, place pineapple slices on grill to add grill marks and golden edges.

When the chicken is done serve hot topped with the pineapple slices.

Tailgate Friendly

Smoky Tailgate Spicy Wings

The secret to this recipe is the overnight marinade for a deep smoked flavor with a spicy bite. I generally say chicken and other delicate meats don't require a long marinade time...but this is an exception.

SMOKE AND HEAT MARINADE:

½ cup barbecue sauce

½ cup apple cider vinegar

½ (4-ounce) bottle liquid smoke seasoning (4 tablespoons)

2 tablespoons hot sauce

1 tablespoon minced garlic

24 chicken wings

GRILLING SPICES:

2 tablespoons garlic salt

1 tablespoon cayenne pepper

1 tablespoon cumin powder

½ tablespoon chili powder

½ tablespoon paprika

Dash black pepper

1 tablespoon brown sugar

Combine marinade ingredients in a bowl and mix well. Toss to coat chicken wings. Cover and chill overnight. Stir a few times to keep things evenly mixed and coated.

Get your grill going and remove chicken from marinade. (Discard marinade.) Grill chicken over medium-high heat while turning as needed.

Sprinkle Grilling Spices on wings as they cook. When done, remove wings from grill; give them another light sprinkle of seasoning. Serve hot.

For Spices: Place all in a bowl, zip-close bag or shaker; mix well.

A PRINTER, A PHARMACIST, AND LIQUID SMOKE.

Have you ever wondered how Liquid Smoke is made? Well, turns out that it's really smoke, caught in a liquid. As a kid working in a print shop, Ernest H. Wright noticed black liquid dripping from a stove pipe. Years later, Wright was a pharmacist and decided to turn what he witnessed as a child into a product. He used a wood fire and passed the smoke through a tube into a condenser. When the smoke was in the condenser it cooled and formed a liquid much like the black liquid he witnessed as a child. So how did a pharmacist in the 1800's test a new food flavoring? Wright simply prepared a ham using his new "Condensed Smoke" invention and fed it to his friends. They like it so he perfected it and started selling his product in 1895.

Serious Grilling

Zesty Grilled Cheater Wings

This recipe is so easy, it's like cheating.

24 mini wings and drums

¾ cup zesty Italian dressing

¾ cup barbecue sauce

Hot sauce to taste

½ green bell pepper, minced

½ small onion, minced

2 tablespoons parsley flakes

Marinate chicken in mixture of Italian dressing, barbecue sauce, hot sauce, bell pepper, onion and parsley. Cover; chill for a couple of hours.

Grill over high heat until juices run clear. (You can also bake the wings in the oven at 350° on a cookie sheet treated with nonstick spray until juices run clear and wings are golden.)

Basic Hot & Buttery Grilled Wings

24 mini wings and drums

Black pepper to taste

1 cup hot sauce

2 sticks butter, melted

Dash garlic powder

Sprinkle wings with black pepper (not much; just a few dashes).

Combine hot sauce, butter and garlic powder in a bowl. Either toss wings in mixture or brush wings with sauce as you grill them.

Grill over high heat, basting and turning as needed, until juices run clear. (You can also bake wings in the oven at 350° on a cookie sheet treated with nonstick spray until juices run clear and wings are golden.)

Apricot Ginger Ale Whole Wings

This recipe is for whole chicken wing sections, but you can easily use wings and drummies.

12 whole chicken wings

1 (12-ounce) can ginger ale

½ cup soy sauce

2 garlic cloves, minced

Dash ginger powder

Salt and pepper to taste

1 (10-ounce) jar apricot
  preserves

Lay chicken wings in a glass baking dish or large plastic dish with cover.

Combine ginger ale, soy sauce, garlic, ginger, salt and pepper in a medium bowl and mix well. Pour over chicken and refrigerate at least 3 hours or overnight, turning from time to time.

Prepare grill for direct grilling over medium-high heat. While grill is getting going, heat preserves in a bowl in microwave (or in a saucepan on stove). Heat just until preserves liquefy slightly.

Remove wings from container and discard marinade. Grill 25 to 30 minutes, turning as needed. During last few minutes of grilling, baste wings heavily with apricot preserves.

THAT'S A BUNCH OF WINGS!

The National Chicken Council stated in its 2016 "Wing Report" that Americans would consume 162.5 million pounds chicken wings during the Super Bowl. That equals 1.3 billion wings which was an increase of 3%, or 37.5 million wing, increase from the previous year. According to the Council that is enough for every single person in the U.S.—man, woman, and child—to enjoy four wings each.

Source: The National Chicken Council

Serious Grilling

Grilled Barbecue & Tennessee Whiskey Honey Wings

I'm from Tennessee but was born in Kentucky so I appreciate both Tennessee Whiskey and Kentucky Bourbon. This recipe is delicious and versatile – it tastes great with either.

24 chicken wings and drummies

1 cup barbecue sauce

2 tablespoons butter, melted

2 to 3 tablespoons Tennessee whiskey or Kentucky bourbon

2 to 3 tablespoons honey

Place chicken in a large bowl.

In a smaller bowl, combine remaining ingredients to make a sauce. Pour half the sauce over chicken and mix to ensure chicken is well coated; reserve remaining sauce in refrigerator. Marinate chicken, covered, in refrigerator several hours.

Before you grill, place reserved half of sauce in a saucepan over medium heat and cook until reduced slightly.

Grill wings over medium-high heat, basting with thickened sauce and turning as needed.

Grilled Salsa Wings

This recipe is a crowd pleaser and perfect for tailgating because it's simple and requires little or no prep time. My only suggestion is stick with a salsa that's not too chunky.

24 chicken wings and drummies

¼ cup honey

2 tablespoons lime or lemon juice

1 (16-ounce) jar salsa (hot or mild)

Place wings in a foil pan and drizzle with honey, lime juice and salsa.

Place pan over medium-high heat and start grilling. If you want grill marks, move the wings back and forth between the foil pan (for basting) and the hot grill grates (for grill marks). Cook until done and serve hot. (Discard any remaining salsa left in pan.)

Cherry Dr. Pepper Slow Smoked Turkey Breasts, Legs and Wings

Ron Ellis is a grilling and barbecue guru. He and his wife Ginger are also United States Coast Guard Auxiliary Food Service Specialists (AUXFS) and helped develop a nationwide program to train USCG Auxiliary members in the fine art of culinary skills. When not training cooks for the Coast Guard, the couple run Ginger Hill Bed and Breakfast in Virginia. Here's Ron's method for slow smoking a turkey.

1 turkey

1 gallon water

1 cup kosher salt

1 cup brown sugar

¾ cup Dizzy Pig Dizzy Dust (or rub seasoning), divided

2 tablespoons olive oil

2 (12-ounce) cans Cherry Dr. Pepper

Cut turkey in pieces as you would a chicken.

Combine water, kosher salt, brown sugar and ½ cup Dizzy Dust; add turkey and refrigerate 8 hours or overnight.

Rinse turkey pieces, pat dry and rest on counter about 30 minutes.

In a small bowl, combine remaining ¼ cup Dizzy Dust with olive oil. Rub mixture all over turkey.

Set up your covered grill for offset smoking or use a smoker. Smoke at 240° for 30 to 35 minutes per pound.

Pour Cherry Dr. Pepper in a drip pan below turkey. Baste turkey 2 or 3 times during smoke time. Remove turkey when internal temperature reaches 165°.

Rest 15 to 20 minutes before carving. Enjoy!

Supporting Norfolk, VA Harborfest by providing meals for CG, CGAux., LE, Fire and rescue.

Serious Grilling

Whole Smoked Brown Sugar Brined Turkey

My best tip for this recipe — don't buy a turkey too large for your smoker.
Also, plan a day ahead for brining.

BRINING:

1 (10- to 12-pound) turkey, thawed, neck and giblets removed

1 cup brown sugar

½ cup salt

2 to 3 tablespoons cayenne pepper

COOKING:

Olive oil

Garlic powder to taste

Salt and pepper to taste

1 small onion, quartered

1 orange (or lemon), quartered

1 stick butter, melted

Place turkey in a stockpot with cold water to cover; add brown sugar, salt and cayenne pepper. Refrigerate overnight.

Remove turkey from brine, allowing excess liquid to drain; place in a heavy-duty foil roasting pan. (Discard brine.)

Rub turkey with olive oil and sprinkle on garlic powder, salt and pepper to taste. Place onion and orange in turkey cavity.

You can cook on a smoker with offset heat and hickory smoke, or use offset grilling method on rectangle covered grill. You're looking for a cooking chamber temperature of about 250°.

Use a drip pan with water placed directly under your bird. Smoke time will be 3½ to 4 hours. If using a grill, cook time will probably need to be increased. About an hour before bird is done, brush it down with butter. Cook to an internal temperature of 165° taken with a thermometer in the deepest part of the bird.

STUFF ON A STICK

WHAT IS A KABOB?

The short answer...kabob is stuff on a stick cooked over a heat source...but that's way too simple. Kabob, or kebab, has deep roots in the Middle East and Mediterranean...oh, and southern regions of Asia. It seems people across many parts of the globe figured out early on that you could cook stuff on a stick over a flame without getting burned. The kabob is so old that it's actually mentioned in Homer's Odyssey. Add some seasoning and sauce and suddenly you have barbecue kabobs.

Many regions have different names for stuff on a stick.
Here are a few: City Chicken (USA), Brochette (France), Souvlaki (Greece), Shashlik (Russia), Satay (parts of Southern Asia), Yakitori (Japan), Chuan (China), Shish Kebab (Turkey).

TYPES OF KABOB SKEWERS: Kabob skewers are typically made either from wood or stainless steel and may have a handle on one end.

Metal kabob skewers are durable, can sustain the weight of heavier foods such as beef and are often easy to slide food on and off. But they can become extremely hot during cooking.

Wooden or bamboo kebab skewers have the advantage of being inexpensive and disposable. A disadvantage is that the skewer may splinter or crack during the preparation and cooking of food. Diners may also experience difficulty sliding food off wooden skewers. Prior to grilling, wooden skewers must be soaked in water for about 10 minutes to avoid burning.

Serious Grilling

Asian Steakhouse Ribeye Steak and Mushroom Kabobs

Get flavor you love from an Asian steakhouse right on the grill in your own back yard.

1½ pounds ribeye steak, cubed

Assorted sliced vegetables of your choice

½ cup soy sauce

3 tablespoons dry white wine

3 tablespoons lemon juice

2 tablespoons vegetable oil

½ teaspoon ground ginger

½ teaspoon garlic powder

¼ teaspoon onion powder

Salt and pepper to taste

20 plus small to medium whole mushrooms, rinsed and dried

Combine all ingredients, except mushrooms, in a bowl. Stir gently to coat, cover and chill 2 hours.

Before placing on skewers, add mushrooms and stir to coat. Waiting to add mushrooms helps to keep them from becoming too mushy.

Place everything on skewers, alternating meat and vegetables; cook on a preheated grill over medium-high heat. Grill 8 to 10 minutes, turning as needed, until steak is cooked. Serve hot over rice.

Grilled Water Chestnuts: A nice addition is to toss a can of drained and sliced water chestnuts on the grill. Use a piece of foil or a grilling tray and hit them with some nonstick spray or butter. Drizzle slightly with a soy or teriyaki sauce as you grill.

Serve kabobs and grilled water chestnuts over a bed of rice.

Skewered Asian Grilled Beef Strips

This is my go-to recipe for tougher cuts of steaks. The trick is to tenderize the beef with a meat hammer as well as using an overnight marinade. You can buy steaks already in strips or cut your own. You're looking for beef strips you can place on a skewer, so don't go too thick.

1 pound steak or steak strips

½ cup red wine vinegar

⅓ cup soy sauce

2 tablespoons olive oil

1 tablespoon brown sugar

½ tablespoon minced garlic

¼ teaspoon oregano

Slice steaks and tenderize using a hammer-style or bladed-style meat tenderizer. Place strips in a glass baking dish (or heavy duty zip-close bag).

Combine remaining ingredients in a bowl and pour over steak strips. Cover (or seal) and refrigerate overnight, turning occasionally. Remove strips from marinade and boil remaining mixture in a saucepan with ¼ cup water.

Thread steak on skewers. Place skewers on grill over high heat and grill to medium well, basting with boiled marinade. (This should only take a few minutes on the grill. Don't overcook or meat may get tough.) Serve hot.

Serious Grilling

Red Wine Vinaigrette Sirloin Steak Kabobs

It's a hearty grilled steak dinner on a stick.

MARINADE:

½ cup red wine vinaigrette

½ cup Worcestershire sauce

1 tablespoon lime juice

1 tablespoon thyme

2 teaspoons black pepper

2 teaspoons garlic powder

KABOBS:

2 pounds beef sirloin steak,
    1½-inch cubes

1 large red onion, wedge cut
    1½-inch pieces

2 medium bell peppers,
    1½-inch pieces

2½ cups wedged potatoes

Mushroom caps or thick slices

Combine Marinade ingredients in a large bowl and mix well. Add beef cubes and stir to coat. Cover and chill at least 1 hour or longer. Stir occasionally while marinating.

When you're ready to cook, remove beef cubes from marinade. Heat marinade in a microwave or saucepan to a quick boil while building kabobs.

Thread beef cubes, onion pieces, bell pepper pieces, potato wedges and mushrooms onto wood or metal skewers.

Grill kabobs over medium-high heat on a preheated grill. Cook 10 to 15 minutes or until beef is cooked to your desired doneness. Turn as needed and baste with cooked marinade. Allow to rest a few minutes before serving.

GRILL TALK: Do you like your steak and veggies separate? That might help with grilling times if you have a thick steak. So, grill the veggies on a separate kabob than your steak.

Grilled Lime Steak Kabobs with Caramelized Sweet Onion Relish

This easy grilling recipe packs a bunch of flavor.

1½ pounds top sirloin steak, 1 to 1½ inches thick

1 lime, juiced

Salt and pepper to taste

Garlic pepper seasoning to taste

CARAMELIZED SWEET ONION RELISH:

2 tablespoons olive oil

1 sweet onion, diced

1 red bell pepper, diced

1 (8.75-ounce) can whole-kernel corn, drained

½ cup balsamic vinegar

¼ cup packed brown sugar

Salt and pepper to taste

If using wood or bamboo skewers, be sure to soak them in water at least 10 minutes.

Marinate beef in lime juice, salt, pepper and garlic pepper.

While skewers are soaking and meat is marinating, prepare the Caramelized Sweet Onion Relish.

Place meat on skewers and grill over medium-high heat, turning as needed, until medium well, 8 to 10 minutes. Serve finished kabobs topped with Caramelized Sweet Onion Relish (or serve relish on the side).

For Relish: Heat olive oil in a nonstick skillet over medium heat. Add onion, pepper and corn; sauté until slightly tender.

Add balsamic vinegar, brown sugar and salt and pepper to taste. Cook about 5 more minutes or until excess liquid evaporates and relish thickens. Any leftover relish makes a great dip for bagel chips.

Serious Grilling

Louisiana Beef Creole Brochette

There's no denying the heavy French influence along parts of the South, especially in South Carolina and Louisiana. That's why there's a good chance the meat and veggies served up on a skewer will be called a "brochette" instead of a kabob. Brochette is French for skewer.

1½ pounds top sirloin, 1 inch cubed

2 cloves garlic, minced

1 onion, sliced

2 red or yellow bell peppers, sliced

1 tablespoon cilantro flakes

1 lemon, juiced

2 to 3 tablespoons plain yogurt

2 tablespoons Creole seasoning

1 tablespoon steak sauce

2½ teaspoons olive oil

Dash ginger power

Dash celery powder

Salt and pepper to taste

Combine all ingredients in a bowl, toss or stir to coat, cover and chill several hours.

Place on skewers and grill over medium-high heat, turning as needed, about 10 minutes or to your desired temperature. Serve hot off the grill.

Stuff on a Stick

Beer and Barbecue Meat Lovers Kabob

MARINADE:

1 (12-ounce) can beer

⅓ cup soy sauce

⅓ cup steak sauce

2 tablespoons barbecue sauce

Garlic powder to taste

Ginger powder to taste

Salt and pepper to taste

KABOBS:

1 pound tender beef, cubed

1 pound pork steak, cubed

1 pound smoked sausage, thick sliced

1 pound chicken breasts, cubed

2 onions, thick sliced

2 bell peppers, thick sliced

Combine all Marinade ingredients in a large bowl. Add all meat. Mix to coat evenly. Cover and chill 1 to 2 hours.

Place meat and vegetables on soaked wooden (or metal) skewers. Baste with Marinade and sprinkle with additional garlic powder, ginger, salt and pepper.

Grill over medium-high heat (or bake at 375°) until meat is cooked to desired doneness. Serve hot with grilled corn on the cob

NO TIME TO MARINATE?

If you don't have time to marinade, then do this instead. Arrange meat on a cookie sheet, brush with olive oil and sprinkle with salt and pepper (or your favorite seasoning).

In a small bowl, combine ⅔ cup steak sauce and ⅔ cup barbecue sauce with just a little beer to make a thick mixture for basting your kabobs.

Serious Grilling

Grilled Ginger Pork Kabobs with Yum Yum Sauce

These pork kabobs have a tasty Asian flavor and are easy to prepare.

4 large pork steaks or chops

¼ cup oil

¼ cup soy sauce

1 tablespoon ground ginger

1 tablespoon brown sugar

Black pepper, red pepper flakes and salt to taste

Green bell pepper, onions, zucchini and squash, as desired

Yum Yum Sauce (page 98)

Cut pork into 1- to 1½-inch cubes.

Combine with remaining ingredients, except Yum Yum Sauce, in a large bowl (or zip-close bag). Cover bowl (or seal bag) and chill several hours. Turn mixture a few times to evenly coat.

Place all of items on skewers and grill over medium-high to high heat, turning often, until done.

Serve with Yum Yum Sauce.

Apple and Pork Kabobs with White Mustard 'Que Sauce

This recipe is perfect for fall grilling. I prefer flat metal skewers for this recipe as the apple seems to hold up better.

1 pound pork, cubed

1 tablespoon apple cider vinegar

⅓ cup barbecue sauce

2 to 3 apples

½ onion, quartered

Water

Lemon juice

WHITE MUSTARD 'QUE SAUCE:

1½ cups mayonnaise or sour cream

1 cup barbecue sauce

Place pork, cider vinegar and barbecue sauce in a bowl, cover and chill overnight.

Core apples and slice into wedges before you are ready to grill. Keep the skin on as that helps keep the apple intact. Cover apples in water mixed with a little lemon juice to keep them from turning brown while you work.

Thread pork, apple, and onion petals onto flat metal skewers and grill over medium-high heat, turning as needed, until done.

Drizzle with White Mustard 'Que Sauce just before serving.

For Sauce: Mix sour cream and barbecue sauce in a bowl and use as a drizzle sauce.

Boneless Barbecue Pork Chops on a Stick

Tailgate Friendly

1 pound boneless pork chops, thin cut

1 onion

½ cup red wine vinegar

½ cup barbecue sauce

1 tablespoon oil

1 tablespoon brown sugar

1 garlic clove, minced

¼ teaspoon oregano

Slice pork and onion into strips and arrange in a baking dish or zip-close bag.

For marinade, combine vinegar, barbecue sauce, oil, brown sugar, garlic and oregano in a bowl; mix well. Pour over pork strips and mix to coat. Cover and refrigerate overnight or as long as possible, turning occasionally.

Remove pork and onion from marinade and thread on skewers. Put remaining marinade into a small saucepan, add a little water and bring to a boil.

Place skewers on grill over high heat and grill several minutes. Turn and baste with the marinade as needed. Serve hot.

Serious Grilling

Sweet Gingered Five-Spice Pork Kabobs

When slicing your vegetables try to be consistent on the size of the slices. I like to keep items such a carrots and zucchini under an inch.

4 pork steaks, cubed 1 inch

1 onion, sliced

1 large green bell pepper, sliced

1 to 2 carrots, peeled and sliced

1 zucchini, sliced

¼ cup vegetable oil

¼ cup soy sauce

1 tablespoon hoisin sauce

1 tablespoon brown sugar

½ tablespoon five spice seasoning

½ tablespoon ground ginger

2 teaspoons salt

2 teaspoons black pepper

Combine all ingredients in a bowl. Toss to coat evenly. Cover and chill overnight, turning or stirring the mixture occasionally.

Gently place pork and vegetables evenly on prepared skewers. You can cook the marinade to use as a basting sauce while grilling.

Cook over a preheated grill using medium-high to high heat, turning as needed for 8 to 10 minutes or until pork is done and vegetables have browned edges.

Serve hot.

I like to serve these kabobs over a bed of seasoned rice. You can be creative and season plain rice, or buy one of those packages that have the spices included.

Easy Rolled Italian Chicken Kabobs & Mozzarella Garlic Bread

4 boneless chicken breasts

Olive oil

Italian seasoning

Pizza sauce

Pepperoni slices

Shredded mozzarella cheese

MOZZARELLA GARLIC BREAD:

Your choice of bread!

Butter

Italian seasoning

Garlic powder

Shredded mozzarella cheese

Flatten each chicken breast between layers of cling wrap or wax paper using a meat pounder or rolling pin.

Brush the flattened breasts lightly with olive oil on both sides. Sprinkle side facing up with Italian seasoning. Add a small amount of pizza sauce and layer with a few pepperoni slices.

Roll the breast up while being careful to not squeeze all of the sauce out. Once rolled, gently cut into thick slices and place several spirals on each skewer.

Grill over medium high heat, turning as needed. While grilling sprinkle with additional Italian seasoning and baste once or twice with additional pizza sauce.

Sprinkle each kabob with mozzarella cheese while they are hot off the grill.

Serve each kabob on a piece of your toasted Mozzarella Garlic Bread.

For Bread: Butter bread, sprinkle with Italian seasoning, garlic powder and shredded mozzarella cheese. Toast in the oven or heat on the grill.

Bread options are wide open here. You can use French bread, hoagie rolls, or even prepared pizza crusts. Just cut to fit the chicken pieces.

Serious Grilling

Boneless Five Spice Chicken Thighs on a Stick

6 to 8 boneless, skinless chicken thighs

½ cup soy sauce

¼ cup yogurt (any flavor)

½ tablespoon rice wine vinegar

2 teaspoons sunflower oil

½ to 1 tablespoon Homemade Asian Five Spice Seasoning (or store-bought)

HOMEMADE ASIAN FIVE SPICE SEASONING BLEND:

2 teaspoons cinnamon

2 teaspoons ground anise

2 teaspoons ground ginger

2 teaspoons ground nutmeg

2 teaspoons ground clove

Combine all ingredients in a bowl with cover (or zip-close bag). Toss to coat evenly. Cover and chill at least an hour or overnight.

Remove thighs from mixture and place them one at a time onto prepared wood skewers or metal skewers. Boneless thighs lend themselves to being twisted and turned. Try to evenly spread meat across skewers so they cook evenly. Don't worry about breaking the pieces up. Just make sure the chicken is evenly distributed on skewers.

Grill over medium-high to high heat several minutes per side until fully cooked. Serve hot with Asian-style slaw, seasoned rice or mixed green salad.

For Seasoning: Combine all spices in a bowl. Store leftovers in a cool dry place.

Tailgate Friendly

Apricot Preserve Chicken Kabobs

These kabobs are sweet, tangy, sticky and packed with flavor. I suggest making a second batch of the marinade for extra basting or to use as a dipping sauce.

1 cup water

2 chicken bouillon cubes

½ to ⅔ cup apricot preserves

⅓ cup soy sauce

½ tablespoon vegetable oil

½ tablespoon minced garlic

½ tablespoon onion powder

2 teaspoons ginger

2 teaspoons hot sauce

1½ pounds boneless skinless chicken breasts, 1-inch cubes

1 red bell pepper, kabob cut

1 onion, kabob cut

In a saucepan, combine water, bouillon cubes, apricot preserves, soy sauce and oil. Cook over medium heat until preserves thin. Add garlic, onion powder, ginger and hot sauce. Stir to mix well; remove from heat.

Cool mixture, then transfer to a large bowl (or zip-close bag). Add chicken, cover or seal and chill at least an hour up to overnight. Turn occasionally to evenly mix.

Remove chicken from marinade and set aside. Heat remaining marinade in a saucepan to a quick boil; remove from heat. Use to brush kabobs while grilling.

Place chicken, bell pepper and onion on metal or soaked wooden skewers; grill over medium-high heat. Turn, grill, brush and repeat until chicken is cooked through and juices run clear.

If you're looking for a good sauce for all kinds of meats, then whip up a batch of the apricot marinade mixture. Just leave out the chicken, and sliced veggies.

Citrus Kissed Barbecue Chicken Kabobs

Somehow the taste of citrus juice, grilling, and barbecue just seem to fit together. This quick and easy dish is perfect over rice.

4 boneless chicken breasts

Raw vegetables of your choice

⅓ cup honey

½ cup barbecue sauce

2 tablespoons orange juice

1 tablespoon apple cider vinegar

Salt, pepper and garlic powder taste

Cube chicken and set aside. Slice vegetables and set aside.

Combine remaining ingredients in a bowl and mix well. Add chicken and vegetables and turn to coat well.

Put meat and veggies on metal skewers and place on a cookie sheet; baste with sauce.

Cover with foil and chill before grilling. Grill over medium-high heat, turning as you grill, to desired temperature. Serve hot.

Peanut Sauced Chicken on a Stick

8 to 10 chicken tenders

4 tablespoons soy sauce, divided

2 tablespoons lemon (or lime) juice

½ cup creamy peanut butter

1 tablespoon brown sugar

1 tablespoon honey

2 to 3 teaspoons Asian-style chili garlic sauce

Combine chicken tenders in a bowl with 2 tablespoons soy sauce and lemon juice. Coat evenly and set aside.

Combine remaining 2 tablespoons soy sauce, peanut butter, brown sugar, honey and chili sauce in a bowl; mix well.

When ready to grill, place chicken on skewers lengthwise; don't bunch chicken up—stretch it along skewer. Brush chicken with sauce and grill over high heat, turning as needed.

Cook until chicken is done to an internal temperature of 165°, about 6 minutes. Serve hot.

Stuff on a Stick

Grilled Tuna Kabobs

2 to 3 tuna steaks, cubed

⅓ cup extra virgin olive oil

Dash soy sauce

2 teaspoons seafood seasoning

3 tablespoons chopped fresh cilantro

4 limes or lemons, divided

1 large onion, kabob cut

2 yellow or red bell peppers, kabob cut

Salt and cracked black pepper to taste

Combine tuna, oil, soy sauce, seafood seasoning and cilantro in a large bowl. Add juice of 2 limes. Toss to evenly coat, cover and chill about 30 minutes.

Slice remaining 2 limes. Thread tuna, slices of lime, onions and bell peppers onto skewers. Grill over high heat about 2 minutes per side, rotating as needed. Brush with any remaining marinade during first half of grilling process (only). Sprinkle with salt and cracked pepper; serve hot.

NOTE: You can also use shark or other heavier types of seafood for this recipe. Wrap a piece of lemon or lime around pieces that look fragile or when using more delicate types of seafood.

Serious Grilling

Sweet & Spicy Pineapple Shrimp Kabobs

24 medium to large peeled shrimp

2 cups cubed pineapple

½ cup maple syrup

½ tablespoon cumin powder

3 teaspoons cayenne pepper

2 teaspoons seafood seasoning

Heat your grill to medium-high heat. Soak bamboo skewers in water while you prepare fruit.

Combine all ingredients together and stir to coat shrimp and pineapple.

Add fruit and shrimp to skewers and grill a few minutes on each side or until shrimp is fully cooked.

Taste of the Islands Grilled Shrimp and Bacon Skewers

You may need to even out the grilling time between the shrimp and bacon. Here are a couple ways to do this. First, you can use big shrimp that are frozen. Larger shrimp means longer grilling times, which will help cook the bacon a bit more. Or, you can preheat the bacon on a cookie sheet in the oven; don't fully cook them. Cool before placing on skewers. Any drippings can be added to your sauce.

2 (20-ounce) cans pineapple chunks with juice

2 to 3 pounds medium or large shrimp, peeled and deveined

½ to 1 pound bacon, diced

Red bell peppers, kabob cut

Green bell peppers, kabob cut

Onions, kabob cut

Cherry tomatoes

1 cup sweet and sour sauce

Preheat grill for medium-high to high heat. Drain pineapple, reserving juice.

Place shrimp, pineapple chunks, bacon, bell peppers, onions and cherry tomatoes on skewers, alternating as you go. Place skewers on a cookie sheet and set aside.

Combine sweet and sour sauce with reserved pineapple juice and mix well. Evenly baste kabobs with sauce mix before grilling.

Baste often with remaining sauce as you grill, turning as needed.

Six Easy Shrimp Kabobs

Shrimp makes for an easy kabob experience especially with these simple recipes that use only a few ingredients.

EASY BARBECUE SHRIMP KABOBS

Grab some peeled tail-on shrimp, place them on a skewer and baste with barbecue sauce as you grill. Serve them up hot.

EASY CAJUN SHRIMP KABOBS

Place peeled tail-on shrimp on a skewer. Brush with a blend of melted butter and hot sauce while grilling. Sprinkle lightly with Cajun (or Creole) seasoning before serving.

EASY ORANGE SHRIMP KABOBS

Place peeled tail-on shrimp on a skewer. Marinate in orange juice before grilling. Sprinkle with orange zest and thyme before removing from grill.

EASY SWEET AND SOUR SHRIMP KABOBS

Why not grab some of your favorite sweet and sour sauce for your next batch of shrimp kabobs? You can baste the kabobs as you grill or simply season them with butter and soy sauce and serve the sweet and sour sauce on the side.

EASY SEAFOOD BUTTER SHRIMP KABOBS

Place peeled tail-on shrimp on a skewer. Brush with melted butter as they grill and sprinkle with a pepper and seafood seasoning. Quick, easy and full of flavor.

EASY SCALLOP AND SHRIMP KABOBS

Select some kabob-sized scallops to go along with some jumbo shrimp. Cut some of your favorite vegetables into large pieces. Place everything on skewers and grill. Brush kabobs with a mixture of melted butter and lime juice. Then sprinkle with seafood seasoning before removing from grill.

Serious Grilling

Quick and Easy Vegetable Kabobs

The sky is the limit for ingredients and seasonings you can use for these kabobs as different items come into season.

2 cups cauliflower florets

2 cups broccoli florets

1 cucumber, cubed into 1-inch pieces

1 red bell pepper, sliced into 1-inch pieces

1 sweet onion, sliced into 1-inch pieces

Carrots, peeled and sliced into 1-inch pieces

1 (8-ounce) bottle zesty Italian dressing

Place vegetables on skewers and arrange in a glass baking dish. Brush with dressing and chill while grill is heating up.

Grill over medium-high heat just long enough to add grill marks and soften slightly. Turn as needed. I like to serve with a little crunch left in the vegetables. The longer you grill the softer the veggies will become so grill to your desired tenderness.

The non-grilled version: These kabobs are also wonderful if you don't grill them. Just save the zesty Italian dressing for a dipping sauce. Serve chilled as a side salad on a stick.

Canned Cajun Tater Tailgate Kabobs

Here's a quick and easy tailgate recipe from my racing days that translates perfectly to any grilling session.

2 (15½-ounce) cans whole white potatoes, drained and rinsed

Vegetable oil

Salt and pepper to taste

Garlic powder to taste

Cajun seasoning to taste

Place potatoes on skewers. Place on a cookie sheet and brush with vegetable oil. Sprinkle with salt, pepper, garlic powder and Cajun seasoning. Roll and rotate kabobs while you sprinkle to cover all sides.

Grill over a preheated medium-high grill 8 to 10 minutes. Rotate and turn as needed. Allow kabobs to become golden with slight grill marks.

Easy additions: Serve hot sprinkled with shredded cheese, if desired, or add pieces of smoked sausage, kielbasa or knackwurst for an Oktoberfest dish with a Cajun kick.

6

Quick Kid-Friendly Kabobs

Don't forget the kids (or kids at heart) when it comes to meals on a stick.

PEANUT BUTTER & JELLY KABOBS

Make some peanut and butter and jelly sandwiches and cut them into four pieces. Stick them on a skewer and you have a kid friendly kabob. You can also use just about any sandwich your kids enjoy. Why not a ham sandwich kabob, a BLT kabob, or even a hamburger slider kabob?

FRUIT KABOBS

We all know what types of fruit our children enjoy. Why not combine them on a skewer? Add a fruit dipping sauce and they might even eat different kinds of fruit. Add whipped cream for a quick dessert.

VEGGIE KABOBS

The secret here is letting your kids and young guests do the selecting. Let them pick the veggies they want on their skewer. Some ranch dipping sauce on the side makes it perfect. Who knows...you might even be able to toss some veggie kabobs on the grill.

HOT DOG KABOBS

Why not a sliced hot dog kabob? You can add other links such as sausage and bratwursts slices. Grill them up and let the kids add the bun and favorite toppings.

MEATBALL KABOBS

Make homemade meatballs or use frozen and thawed store-bought meatballs for yummy meatball kabobs. Who knows, you might even be able to sneak in a few vegetables, such as green bell peppers, onion and more. Brush on some marina or pizza sauce for added flavor.

DELI CHEESE & PEPPERONI KABOBS:

Check out your local deli for kid-friendly kabob ideas. Combine cube deli cheese and pepperoni slices with assorted items such as olives, pickles and more.

Serious Grilling

Grilled Fruit and Yogurt Kabobs

4 cups cubed favorite fruit

1 lime, juiced

1 cup yogurt (plain or flavored)

2 tablespoons honey

Place fruit on skewers and set on a cookie sheet. Drizzle with lime juice.

In a bowl, combine yogurt and honey. Brush over each kabob. Grill on a preheated grill over high heat for 2 to 3 minutes per side—just enough to add grill marks and lightly brown edges. Serve right off the grill.

The non-grilled version: These kabobs are also wonderful even if you don't grill them. Use the yogurt sauce as a dipping sauce. Serve chilled.

Stuff on a Stick

SEAFOOD ON THE BARBIE

DON'T SHY AWAY FROM SEAFOOD ON THE GRILL.

The main thing to realize is that seafood is more tender than steak or pork. So, you will want to use foil, a grilling basket or grilling tray and coat it with nonstick spray. This keeps your selection from sticking to the grill grates. Trust me, once you use a grilling basket that you can flip in a snap with no worries of the meat falling apart, you'll be hooked.

A COUPLE OF FISH AND SEAFOOD GRILLING NOTES:

- Turn fish fillets as few times as possible to avoid breaking up delicate varieties. As I said, a grilling basket works wonders.

- Always marinate seafood in a refrigerator. Marinades for most seafood fillets should be used for an hour or less. I generally stick to 30 minutes or less for delicate fillets and longer for seafood steaks and heartier cuts.

- I like to cook seafood fillets, and the majority of seafood steaks, over medium-high heat. This allows for even cooking and helps keep the meat moist, tender and flaky. On the other hand, I prefer higher grilling temperatures for shell fish, shrimp and lobster.

  - Citrus juice is a great seasoning for just about any fillet.

  - Use a fork or butter knife to gently lift fillet away from grill grates. Then slide your spatula under fish fillet to turn.

  - Fish, like other foods, will continue to cook slightly after removed from the heat source.

Serious Grilling

Coconut Marinated Shrimp with Piña Colada Sauce

This Piña Colada Sauce is also great for steamed, baked and fried versions of Coconut Shrimp.

2 pounds shrimp, peeled and deveined

⅔ cup coconut water

¼ cup citrus juice (orange, lemon or lime)

2 teaspoons seafood seasoning

Toasted coconut flakes

Melted butter or spray butter

PIÑA COLADA SAUCE:

1 cup sour cream

⅓ cup piña colada liquid drink mix

⅓ cup shredded coconut

Dash hot sauce

Combine shrimp, coconut water, juice and seafood seasoning in a glass bowl (or a zip-close bag) stirring to coat shrimp. Chill 1 hour before grilling.

While shrimp are marinating, toast coconut flakes in 400° oven 5 to 6 minutes or until lightly toasted.

Grill shrimp using a grilling basket or tray over medium-high heat. Turn to cook evenly.

Before removing from the grill, lightly baste, or spray, shrimp with butter and immediately top with toasted coconut flakes.

Drizzle with Piña Colada Sauce or serve it on the side for dipping.

For Sauce: Combine all ingredients in a bowl and chill slightly before serving.

Seafood on the Barbie

Cape San Blas Shrimp Tacos with a Coconut Chili Sauce

Ally and I first cooked these during a vacation to Cape San Blas when a storm washed out the road and we were forced to make dinner from stuff in the fridge.

2 cups lemon yogurt

1 (1.25-ounce) package taco seasoning mix, divided

1 cup coconut milk

1 tablespoon lemon juice

½ cup honey

2 teaspoons brown sugar

½ cup chopped cilantro plus more for topping

1 tablespoon ketchup

2 pounds large shrimp, peeled and deveined

Taco shells

Taco toppings (lettuce or cabbage or coleslaw, tomatoes, cilantro, etc.)

In a bowl, combine yogurt, ¾ tablespoon taco seasoning, coconut milk, lemon juice, honey, brown sugar, cilantro and ketchup to make Coconut Chili Sauce.

Divide in half, placing each in a bowl or zip-close bag. Refrigerate 1 bowl to be used when serving. Add shrimp and remaining taco seasoning to second bowl. Refrigerate 2 hours or longer.

When ready to cook, remove shrimp from marinade (discard marinade). Grill shrimp over medium-high heat. Serve in hard or soft taco shells with your favorite taco toppings and reserved Coconut Chili Sauce on the side.

Quick and Easy Sweet and Spicy Barbecue Grilled Shrimp

20 jumbo shrimp, shelled and deveined

⅓ cup barbecue sauce

2 tablespoons honey

2 tablespoons hot sauce

1½ tablespoons Worcestershire sauce

1 tablespoon lime juice

Salt and pepper to taste

Combine all ingredients in a glass bowl or zip-close bag. Cover or seal and chill 1 hour.

Use a grilling tray (or several sheets of heavy-duty foil folded with edges to create a lip similar to a cookie sheet) prepped with nonstick spray. Pour entire mixture of shrimp and sauce onto the tray.

As shrimp cooks, stir and turn to cook evenly. Sauce will reduce and coat shrimp with a glaze of spicy barbecue sauce. Cook until shrimp are done and opaque. Serve hot.

Easy Grilled Citrus Shrimp

4 cups peeled and deveined medium to large shrimp

1 cup orange juice

½ teaspoon chili powder

Dash ginger

Dash onion powder

Dash garlic powder

1 teaspoon salt

2 teaspoons oregano or Italian seasoning

Parsley

Marinate shrimp in mixture of orange juice, chili powder, ginger, onion powder and garlic powder in zip-close bag or lidded container for about 2 hours, chilled.

Prepare grill for medium-high heat. Place shrimp on grill (discard marinade) in a grilling basket and top with spray butter. Grill just until shrimp turn pink and edges are slightly browned.

Sprinkle with salt, Italian seasoning and parsley. Serve hot with your choice of sides.

VARIATION: Don't stop with orange juice! You can use all kinds of citrus juice for this recipe including the combination of some of your favorites.

Butter Grilled Shrimp and Homemade Cajun Nacho Chips with Easy Seafood Sauce

Tailgate Friendly

The title of this recipe may be long but the recipe is actually simple and quick...and delicious.

CAJUN NACHO CHIPS:

6 to 8 corn tortillas

Spray butter

Cajun seasoning

EASY SEAFOOD SAUCE:

2½ tablespoons lemon juice

½ cup sugar

1 bottle chili sauce

½ cup ketchup

½ tablespoon Worcestershire sauce

½ tablespoon barbecue sauce

Dash hot sauce

BUTTER GRILLED SHRIMP:

½ cup butter, melted

3 tablespoons lemon juice

2 teaspoons chili powder

2 pounds uncooked jumbo shrimp, peeled and deveined

For Chips: Cut tortillas in half. Then, cut each half in 3 equal triangle pieces. Think of a pizza with 6 slices.

Arrange evenly on a nonstick cookie sheet and spritz with spray butter. Sprinkle with Cajun seasoning to taste.

Bake in a preheated 300° oven 8 to 10 minutes or until chips are golden brown. Rotate sheet after about 6 minutes to ensure even cooking.

For Sauce: In a medium bowl, stir together all ingredients; cover and chill until needed.

For Shrimp: In a bowl, combine butter, lemon juice and chili powder. Add shrimp and stir gently to coat.

Grill shrimp using a grilling basket or tray over medium heat for 3 to 5 minutes on each side or until shrimp turn pink. Remove from heat and serve hot with Cajun Nacho Chips and Easy Seafood Sauce.

Serious Grilling

How to Grill Clams

Grilling clams is easy and only takes a few minutes of actual grilling time. The presoak takes a while so add that into your timeline.

STEP ONE:

Buy the freshest clams possible and plan on cooking them soon after purchasing.

STEP TWO:

Place clams in a clean bucket of cold water to rinse dirt and particles; it also causes the clams to expel any sand.

STEP THREE:

Grill clams over medium-high to high heat until shells pop open. Clams that don't open have spoiled and should be discarded.

STEP FOUR:

Before removing from the grill, drizzle with garlic butter or a little lemon juice, using a light touch so you don't overwhelm the clam flavor. Serve hot.

Serious Grilling

How to Grill a Lobster Tail...
The Easy Way

Don't stress over grilling a lobster tail. They can actually be one of the easiest things you'll ever cook on the grill. If you are using frozen lobster make sure they are thawed completely in the fridge before grilling.

STEP ONE:

Light your charcoal or gas grill.

STEP TWO:

Split tail (if not already done by your local market), using a sharp knife on a firm cutting board, by placing, meat side down, on cutting board. Start at the base of the shell where the little tail fins are. Carefully cut shell while butterflying meat.

Don't cut all of the way through, as that tiny bit of meat left acts as a hinge.

STEP THREE:

Baste meat with a little olive oil, salt, pepper and seafood seasoning. I like a hint of Italian seasoning as well. Toss on some parsley flakes for good measure.

STEP FOUR:

Grill lobster, tail meat side down, over medium heat on a greased grate (or use a grilling basket) about 5 minutes. Turn shell side down; grill another 5 minutes. Baste upturned meat with melted butter and a dash of seafood seasoning. Cook to an internal temperature of 135°.

STEP FIVE:

Remove from grill and eat.

Grilling Oysters 101

STEP ONE:

Select fresh oysters. Before cooking, discard any oysters with open shells.

STEP TWO:

Place oysters on a preheated medium-high grill fat-shell-side down. The flat side should be facing up. The fatter bottom acts as a bowl for natural juices.

STEP THREE:

Close lid and check in 3 to 5 minutes. When the oyster shells pop, cook another 3 minutes, but no longer.

STEP FOUR:

Remove oysters carefully with tongs and move them to your working area. Use a sharp knife (or oyster knife) to cut membrane away from the top/flat part of the shell.

STEP FIVE:

Gently twist top shell off, leaving bottom part of the shell with meat and juices.

STEP SIX:

Quickly add your desired topping and serve hot.

THREE GRILLED OYSTER TOPPING SUGGESTIONS:

- Softened butter with garlic and herbs
- Hot sauce with melted butter and lemon juice
- Horseradish

Serious Grilling

Grilled Shark Steak with Dark Beer and Mustard Marinade

½ (12-ounce) bottle dark beer

¼ cup vegetable oil

2 to 3 tablespoons Dijon mustard

1½ teaspoons garlic powder

1 teaspoon salt

1 teaspoon seafood seasoning

Cracked black pepper

2 to 4 shark steaks

Combine all ingredients, except shark steaks, in a glass baking dish to make a marinade; add steaks. Coat evenly, cover and chill about 30 minutes, turning once.

Grill over medium-hot heat, using a grilling basket or well-greased grates, 4 to 5 minutes per side.

THE INNOVATIVE KETTLE GRILL

One problem for many outdoor grilling enthusiasts in the late 1940s and early 1950s was shallow grills that didn't hold heat. Any wind would cause ashes to float around, landing on the food. The end result was often food burned on the outside and not done on the inside. In 1951, George Stephen, a welder at the Weber Brothers Metal Works, started working on a better grill solution with materials typically used to make steel buoys for Chicago's harbor. Stephen later stated he had to do something because he "was smoking up the neighborhood and burning up half of what I cooked." About a year later, the familiar and versatile Weber Kettle Grill with domed lid and vents to help control temperatures and air flow was born.

Cedar Plank Salmon with Pale Ale Peach Barbecue Sauce

4 to 6 salmon fillets

1 (12-ounce) bottle pale ale

Salt and pepper to taste

PALE ALE PEACH BARBECUE SAUCE:

1 cup barbecue sauce

1 to 2 peaches, peeled and chopped

½ cup pale ale

1 tablespoon balsamic vinegar

2 to 3 tablespoons water

Dash pepper

Place fillets in a glass baking dish; cover with pale ale and sprinkle with salt and pepper. Refrigerate until planks are ready.

Place a fillet on a prepped cedar plank and place on a preheated medium grill. (Don't grill at too high of a temperature as plank may dry out and burn.) Grill until fillet flakes easily with a fork. Serve topped with Pale Ale Peach Barbecue Sauce.

For Sauce: Combine sauce ingredients in a saucepan and bring to a boil. Boil about 1 minute, stirring continuously. Reduce heat to low and cook 20 minutes, stirring occasionally, until sauce thickens and peaches cook down.

PREPPING THE CEDAR PLANKS:

Rinse 4 cedar planks with water to remove any wood particles or dust. Next, fill a sink or other large clean container with water and a teaspoon of salt. Submerge planks in water placing a weight on top. (I use a brick inside of a zip-close bag.) Soak planks 1 to 2 hours.

HOW TO COOK ON A CEDAR PLANK:

First, start with a quality plank. Don't use used planks that are treated or processed. Cedar planks for grilling are commonly found in grill and hearth stores, large chain stores, specialty stores and many grocery stores. Place plank in cool water in a clean container or sink. Place a heavy plate, or other weighted and clean object, over planks to keep them under water. As I said in the recipe above, I use an old brick sealed in a zip-close bag. Soak plank at least 30 minutes up to 2 hours. Turn and rotate the planks so all sides soak evenly.

Serious Grilling

Scot and Tonya's Bourbon Glazed Cedar Plank Salmon

This recipe is courtesy of my brother Scot Campbell and his wife Tonya. Tonya has culinary skills way beyond charcoal and hickory chips. Her cakes are legendary and her love of cooking stems from a culinary-loving family. Combine Scot's love of anything on the grill (a trait all of my brothers and I share) and Tonya's knowledge of classical cooking then you can bet the flavors will shine when it's time to light the charcoal.

⅔ cup orange juice

⅓ cup maple syrup

2 tablespoons bourbon

2 tablespoons soy sauce

2 tablespoons light brown sugar

1 tablespoon course-ground mustard

4 salmon fillets

4 cedar planks (prepare per directions on opposite page)

Make bourbon glaze by combining orange juice, maple syrup, bourbon, soy sauce, brown sugar and mustard in a saucepan. Simmer 15 minutes or until slightly thickened. Cool completely.

Reserve ¼ cup bourbon glaze for drizzle. Place one salmon fillet on each cedar plank, baste with bourbon glaze and place on a preheated medium grill.

Grill, basting with bourbon glaze until fillet flakes easily with a fork. Serve hot, drizzled with reserved bourbon glaze.

Easy Soy Sauce Grilled Swordfish Steaks

4 swordfish steaks, 1 inch thick

Salt and pepper to taste

2 tablespoons melted butter

2 tablespoons soy sauce

2½ teaspoons brown sugar

2 teaspoons garlic powder

Sunflower seed oil, optional

Place swordfish steaks on a glass baking dish and sprinkle with salt and pepper on both sides.

Combine remaining ingredients in a bowl using only 2 drops of sunflower seed oil (if you have it on hand). Spread over steaks. Cover in cling wrap and chill about 1 hour. (I would not go much longer than that.)

Grill over medium-high heat, turning once, about 5 minutes each side or to an internal temperature of 145°.

Delicious served with Yum Yum Sauce (page 98).

Serious Grilling

Greek Lemon Garlic Grilled Swordfish Steaks

4 swordfish steaks, about ½ to ¾ inch thick

2 tablespoons olive oil

½ lemon, juiced

½ tablespoon minced garlic

Easy Greek Seasoning

EASY GREEK SEASONING:

1½ tablespoons oregano

1 tablespoon thyme

½ tablespoon basil

½ tablespoon marjoram

½ tablespoon onion powder

2½ teaspoons garlic powder

Dash salt and pepper

Brush swordfish steaks with olive oil and lemon juice; rub gently with minced garlic and sprinkle with Easy Greek Seasoning to taste.

Grill over medium-high heat on grates that have been rubbed with oil. Grill about 5 minutes on each side while basting with additional olive oil and sprinkling with additional seasoning. Cook until swordfish steak is opaque and firmed up and flakes slightly with a fork.

For Seasoning: Combine all the ingredients in a bowl and use in a shaker as needed.

Grilled Lime and Ginger Marinated Tuna Steaks with Pineapple Salsa

Tuna steaks can vary in color from white to pink depending on where they are caught. Any kind of citrus added to a tuna steak is a winner for me. This recipe combines simple ingredients for a tasty marinade as well as a very simple Pineapple Salsa that can be ready in minutes.

2 to 4 tuna steaks, ¾ to 1 inch thick

⅓ cup lime juice (or orange juice)

2 tablespoons vegetable oil

½ tablespoon ground ginger

½ tablespoon minced garlic

Sea salt and freshly ground pepper to taste

Red pepper flakes, optional

PINEAPPLE SALSA:

1 (8-ounce) can chopped pineapple, drained

½ cup finely chopped tomato

½ cup chopped sweet onion

2 tablespoons chopped fresh cilantro (or 1 tablespoon dried cilantro flakes)

2 tablespoons finely chopped jalapeño

2 tablespoons lime juice

1 tablespoon olive oil

Salt and pepper to taste

Place tuna steaks in a glass baking dish. Combine remaining ingredients in a bowl and pour over tuna to coat. Cover and chill 2 hours or longer.

Heat coals or gas grill for medium-high direct heat. Remove fish from marinade (discard marinade) and grill about 4 minutes per side, more or less depending on thickness. Cook to an internal temperature of 145°.

Serve hot topped with Pineapple Salsa.

For Salsa: Combine all ingredients in a bowl and mix well. Refrigerate until ready to serve.

Serious Grilling

Rum Blackened Catfish Nuggets

4 catfish fillets (or 8 catfish nuggets)

⅓ cup citrus-flavored rum

3 teaspoons paprika

1 teaspoon thyme

1 teaspoon onion powder

1 teaspoon garlic powder

½ teaspoon salt

½ teaspoon sugar

½ teaspoon ground red pepper

½ teaspoon black pepper

Place catfish in a glass baking dish (or zip-close bag) and cover with citrus-flavored rum. Cover (or seal bag) and chill 1 hour.

Combine remaining ingredients in a bowl for blackening rub.

Place catfish on a plate and coat with blackening rub. Rub it gently into catfish.

Grill over medium-high heat using a grilling basket or tray coated with nonstick spray. Grill 2 to 3 minutes per side or until catfish flakes easily with fork. Serve hot off the grill.

Serious Grilling

Orange Catfish with Spicy Citrus Chipotle Cocktail Sauce

Catfish is so versatile — it can be grilled, baked, broiled, fried and even used in gumbos and stews. Of course, we are grilling catfish and finishing with a neat spin on cocktail sauce.

ORANGE CATFISH:

4 catfish fillets

½ cup orange juice

2 tablespoons vegetable oil

2 tablespoons soy sauce

1 tablespoon lemon juice

½ tablespoon minced garlic

Salt and pepper to taste

SPICY CITRUS CHIPOTLE COCKTAIL SAUCE:

½ cup prepared sweet chili sauce

½ cup ketchup

¼ cup orange juice

3 teaspoons prepared horseradish

2½ teaspoons chipotle chili powder

2 teaspoons seafood seasoning

1½ teaspoons coarse salt

1½ teaspoons cracked black pepper

Place fillets in a glass baking dish (or zip-close bag). Combine remaining ingredients in a bowl to make a marinade; mix well. Coat catfish with marinade, cover and chill 30 minutes.

When ready to cook, remove fillets from marinade and set aside. Boil marinade in a saucepan about 5 minutes.

Grill catfish over medium-high heat about 5 minutes each side, 8 to 10 minutes total grilling time. Lightly baste fillets with boiled marinade.

Serve hot with Spicy Citrus Chipotle Cocktail Sauce on the side.

For Sauce: Combine all ingredients in a glass bowl and mix well. Cover and chill before serving.

Scott's Grilled Catfish and Tropical Fruit Salsa

1 teaspoons minced garlic

½ teaspoon kosher salt

½ teaspoon ground black pepper

¼ teaspoon crushed red pepper

4 catfish fillets

2 tablespoons olive oil

TROPICAL FRUIT SALSA:

1 cup diced mango

1 tablespoon chopped fresh cilantro

1 tablespoon minced jalapeño

2 tablespoons fresh lime juice

1 tablespoon honey

Combine garlic, salt, black pepper and red pepper. Brush each fillet with oil and sprinkle with spice mixture.

Grill until fish flakes easily with a fork. Serve with salsa.

For Salsa: Combine all ingredients in a glass bowl, cover and chill before serving.

Serious Grilling

Grilled Halibut with Sesame Sunflower White Sauce

Halibut is a lean fish known for its mild flavor and firm texture. Because it is so lean, it can dry out quickly so don't overcook.

2 to 4 halibut fillets, about ¾ inch thick

1 tablespoon oil

Kosher salt to taste

Cracked black pepper to taste

Chili powder to taste

Butter, melted

SESAME SUNFLOWER WHITE SAUCE:

½ cup mayonnaise

1 tablespoon rice vinegar

2 teaspoons soy sauce

2 teaspoons sugar

½ teaspoon salt

1 tablespoon sunflower seeds, toasted

Brush fish lightly with oil; sprinkle with salt and pepper and a light dash of chili powder.

Grill fillets 3 to 4 minutes each or until opaque and flakes easily with a fork. While cooking, baste lightly with butter.

Serve fish hot topped with Sesame Sunflower White Sauce.

For Sauce: Combine all ingredients in a glass bowl and chill before serving.

Grilled Tequila Lime Mahi-Mahi

4 skinless mahi-mahi fillets

1 lime, juiced

Salt and pepper to taste

TEQUILA LIME MARINADE:

½ cup finely chopped onion

½ cup lime juice

¼ cup orange juice

¼ cup tequila

1 tablespoon olive oil

½ tablespoon minced jalapeño

Dash chili powder

Dash brown sugar

Rub fillets with lime juice, salt and pepper. Set aside to soak while making Marinade.

Place fillets in a glass baking dish and cover with Marinade. Lift fillets to coat underside. Cover and chill 1 hour.

When ready to grill, remove fish and microwave Marinade 4 minutes to use as a baste.

Place fillets on a preheated grill over medium-high heat using a grilling basket, if desired, basting with cooked Marinade. Grill 3 to 4 minutes per side, turning gently.

Serve hot with your favorite sides and topped with mild salsa or a spicy tartar sauce.

For Marinade: Combine all in a glass bowl.

Grilled Sea Bass Fillets with Garlic Red Potatoes

Start the potatoes first and let them cook while the fillets are on the grill.

4 to 6 sea bass fillets

2 tablespoons melted butter

1 teaspoon olive oil

2 teaspoons paprika

1 teaspoon minced garlic

1 teaspoon thyme

½ teaspoon black pepper

½ teaspoon cayenne pepper

½ teaspoon lemon zest

GARLIC RED POTATOES:

1½ pounds small red potatoes, halved or quartered with skins

2 tablespoons olive oil

Italian seasoning to taste

Garlic salt to taste

Paprika to taste

Place fillets in a glass baking dish. Combine melted butter with olive oil; brush over fish.

Combine remaining ingredients in a small bowl. Sprinkle about half over fillets.

Grill over medium-high heat turning once or twice at the most until done. While fillet is cooking, baste with remaining butter mixture and sprinkle with remaining seasoning.

Serve hot with Garlic Red Potatoes.

For Potatoes: Halve smaller potatoes and quarter larger ones. Combine potatoes and olive oil in a zip-close bag. Shake to coat.

Add seasonings to taste and shake to coat. Spread potatoes on a nonstick cooking sheet and bake in a preheated oven at 375° about 15 minutes. Check for doneness and cook a few more minutes if needed.

Something
EXTRA

MARINADES MADE SIMPLE

LOVE ME TENDER

In general, marinades are designed to tenderize meat by breaking down the fiber of the meat using an acid such as citrus juice or vinegar or with a seasoning such as salt. Marinades can also add flavor, and are used before grilling.

SAFETY WITH MARINADES

Here are few safety tips to keep in mind when using any marinade.

- Marinate meat in a glass or food-safe plastic bowl with a lid. Avoid metal or ceramic bowls or dishes because the acidic property of the marinade will cause a chemical reaction with the metal and with the lead and other particles found in ceramic glazes.

- Raw meat of any type may contain harmful bacteria that may contaminate the marinade. So when you use marinade be sure to avoid cross contamination and not mix your meats in the same marinade.

- Discard any leftover marinade when finished. Or bring it to a boil for several minutes before using for basting or as a sauce.

Something Extra

Eli's Easy Italian Dressing Marinade

This is the first marinade my dad taught me how to make. In truth a bottle of zesty Italian dressing is the perfect start to simple marinade for chicken and pork. This recipe just adds on to that a little bit.

1 cup zesty Italian dressing

½ cup soy sauce

¼ cup Worcestershire sauce

2 tablespoons apple cider vinegar

Mix everything in a glass bowl and cover. Chill before using.

Greek Yogurt Seafood and Chicken Marinade

Yogurt is a great choice for marinating fragile meats, such as fish fillets, other seafood and chicken. Enzymes in the yogurt help tenderize the meat without overpowering it. You can use plain yogurt, Greek yogurt or flavored yogurt.

1 cup Greek yogurt

1 tablespoon dried cilantro

2 tablespoons fresh lemon juice

1 tablespoon minced garlic

1 teaspoon cayenne pepper

1 teaspoon cumin

Kosher salt to taste

Black pepper to taste

Combine all in a blender and mix well. Marinate your meat, covered and chilled, about 30 minutes (seafood) to an hour (chicken).

Citrus Teriyaki Marinade

½ cup soy sauce

½ cup orange juice

¼ cup brown sugar

1½ tablespoons minced garlic

½ teaspoon black pepper

2 teaspoons ginger

2 teaspoons crushed red pepper

Mix everything in a glass bowl and cover. Chill before using.

Hard Cider Marinade

1 cup apple cider vinegar

½ cup beer

¼ cup ketchup

1 tablespoon cayenne pepper

½ tablespoon salt

½ tablespoon sugar

1 tablespoon black pepper

Combine all ingredients in a glass bowl. Cover and chill before using.

Something Extra

Pale Ale and Orange Juice Marinade

I've used this marinade mostly for pork chops, ribs, chicken and seafood such as shrimp and lobster.

1 (12-ounce) can pale ale

½ cup orange juice

¼ cup apple cider vinegar

1 tablespoon brown sugar

2 tablespoons cayenne pepper

1 tablespoon crushed red pepper

1 tablespoon lemon juice

Dash each: thyme, basil, salt and pepper

Mix well and use as a marinade. If marinating pork and beef, refrigerate at least 3 hours or overnight. For chicken, refrigerate about 2 hours. I suggest a marinating time of about 30 minutes for seafood. I also use this to baste lobster and tuna steaks on the grill.

Dark Beer Marinade

This marinade is perfect for beef and pork.

1 (12-ounce) bottle dark beer

⅓ cup minced onion

⅓ cup chopped mushrooms

2 tablespoons bottled teriyaki sauce

1 tablespoon brown sugar

Salt and pepper to taste

Combine all ingredients in a saucepan and bring to a boil for 2 to 3 minutes. Reduce heat to low, cover and simmer until onion is soft.

Hawaiian Pineapple Marinade

Anytime you use pineapple in a recipe, you can count on me eating a bunch. I love the flavor of pineapple, and this marinade can make any meat fantastic.

1 (20-ounce) can pineapple chunks, with juice

⅓ cup ketchup

2 tablespoons soy sauce

1 tablespoon minced garlic

¼ cup chopped onion

1 tablespoon honey

Salt and pepper to taste

Mix everything in a saucepan and simmer about 5 minutes. Cool and process in a blender to break up pineapple chunks. Add a splash of water to thin, if needed.

Sweet and Sour Orange Marinade

Try this Asian-inspired marinade on just about anything from beef and pork to chicken and vegetables.

1 orange

⅔ cup honey

⅔ cup red wine vinegar

3 tablespoons soy sauce

2 tablespoons Worcestershire sauce

1 tablespoon sesame oil

2 teaspoons ginger

Zest orange into a small saucepan. Add juice from orange and remaining ingredients. Bring to a boil. Reduce to a low simmer and continue to cook about 5 minutes.

Something Extra

Caribbean-Style Marinade

This marinade has a bit of heat. Be sure to wear protective gloves and even consider using protective eyewear when working with hot peppers.

½ cup orange juice

⅓ cup soy sauce

¼ cup vinegar

2 Scotch bonnet peppers without stems

4 scallions or green onions, chopped

½ cup chopped red onion

2 tablespoons vegetable oil

1 tablespoon thyme

1 tablespoon allspice

1 tablespoon brown sugar

1 tablespoon minced garlic

2 teaspoons salt

2 teaspoons black pepper

1 teaspoon nutmeg

1 teaspoon cinnamon

1 teaspoon ginger

Toss all ingredients in a blender or food processor and pulse until you have a puréed thick liquid. No need to chill or boil—start using as soon as the blending is done.

Marinades Made Simple

RUB IN THE FLAVOR

RUB IT IN...

A rub can be any combination of spices and seasonings... as simple as salt and pepper...or an elaborate combination of spices... Rubs can be in dry form or wet form. Wet rubs include one liquid ingredient along with the dry seasonings to form a seasoned paste. Rub and press the spices onto raw meat with your hands before cooking.

The meat can be marinated in the spice rub for some time for the flavors to incorporate into the food or it can be cooked immediately after it is coated in the rub. The spice rub can be left on or partially removed before cooking.

A WORD OF CAUTION...

Keep your sugar content in mind. High heat grilling may cause sugars to burn and become bitter so rubs with lots of sugar are best for lower heat.

Something Extra

Basic Deck Chef Rub

This is one of my basic rub recipes for pork, beef, ribs, burgers and more.

1½ tablespoons brown sugar

1½ tablespoons paprika

1½ tablespoons salt

1 tablespoon cumin

1 tablespoon garlic powder

1 tablespoon onion powder

1 tablespoon chili powder

2 teaspoons cayenne pepper

2 teaspoons black pepper

Combine all ingredients in a bowl or shaker. Store covered in a dry place.

Indirect Heat Brown Sugar Rub

This recipe is perfect for cooking, grilling, or smoking with indirect heat. Direct or high heat may cause the sugar to burn and become bitter.

6 tablespoons brown sugar

3 tablespoons chili powder

2 tablespoons paprika

1 tablespoon garlic powder

½ tablespoon onion powder

2 teaspoons salt

2 teaspoons cumin powder

1 teaspoon black pepper

1 teaspoon cinnamon

Combine all ingredients in a bowl or shaker. Store covered in a dry place.

Taste of the Border Rub

This rub recipe has a bit of a kick to it and is inspired by my love of Tex-Mex cooking and south of the border flavors.

3 tablespoons paprika

1½ tablespoons salt

¼ cup brown sugar

2 tablespoons cumin powder

1 tablespoon chili powder

½ tablespoon cayenne pepper

2 teaspoons ground pepper

2 teaspoons coriander

Dash crushed red pepper

Combine all ingredients in a bowl or shaker. Store covered in a dry place.

Something Extra

Jerk Chicken Rub

2 tablespoons dried parsley

2 tablespoons dried onion flakes

½ tablespoon crushed red pepper flakes

½ tablespoon garlic powder

½ tablespoon allspice

2 teaspoons ground thyme

2 teaspoons brown sugar

1½ teaspoons salt

1 teaspoon ground nutmeg

½ teaspoon ground cinnamon

Combine all ingredients in a bowl. Place in a spice or coffee grinder and grind to break up larger flakes. Store covered in bowl, or shaker, in a dry place.

Blackening Seasoning / Rub

3 tablespoons paprika

1 tablespoon salt

½ tablespoon onion powder (not onion salt)

½ tablespoon garlic powder (not garlic salt)

3 teaspoons cayenne pepper

3 teaspoons ground white pepper

3 teaspoons ground black pepper

1 teaspoon crushed or ground dried thyme leaves

1 teaspoon crushed or ground dried oregano leaves

Combine all ingredients in a bowl. Place in a spice or coffee grinder and grind to break up larger flakes. Store covered in a bowl, or shaker, in a dry place.

Seafood Seasoning / Rub

This recipe is similar to seafood seasoning from the grocery store. Because I use red pepper flakes and a bay leaf, I always run this through a spice grinder.

3 tablespoons salt

2 tablespoons ground celery seed

2 teaspoons dry mustard powder

2 teaspoons red pepper flakes

1 teaspoon ground black pepper

1 teaspoon ground bay leaves

1 teaspoon paprika

¼ teaspoon ground cloves

¼ teaspoon ground allspice

¼ teaspoon ground ginger

¼ teaspoon ground cardamom

¼ teaspoon ground cinnamon

Combine all ingredients in a bowl. Place in a spice or coffee grinder and grind to break up larger flakes. Store covered in bowl, or shaker, in a dry place.

Something Extra

Spicy Wet Rub

5 green onions, minced

½ tablespoon crushed red pepper

½ tablespoon minced garlic

¼ cup vegetable oil

¼ cup fresh lime juice

2 tablespoons apple cider vinegar

2 tablespoons soy sauce

1 teaspoon thyme

1 teaspoon chili powder

Dash salt and pepper

Combine all ingredients in a blender or food processor and pulse. Use as a wet rub on chicken or other meats.

Sweet Mustard and Beer Wet Rub

⅓ cup yellow mustard

¼ cup beer

¼ cup brown sugar

¼ cup finely chopped onion

1 tablespoon paprika

1 teaspoon soy sauce

Combine dry ingredients in a bowl, cover and chill. Use as a wet rub on pork, beef or other meats.

SAUCED UP SAUCES

BARBECUE SAUCE:

There are several types of barbecue sauces ranging from simple vinegar-based Carolina styles to mustard-based, sweet sauces, spicy versions and even Alabama white barbecue sauces. A barbecue sauce is often used as a basting sauce, finishing sauce while grilling or as a dipping and drizzle sauce served on the side. The main thing to remember about any barbecue sauce is that they are not marinades, so won't tenderize the meat.

MOP:

Barbecue mops are a combination of liquids and spices that are "mopped" onto food several times during the cooking process. Most often used with smokers and offset grilling, the whole point is to keep the food moist and the cooking chamber from becoming too dry during the "low-and-slow" cooking process.

Something Extra

Grenada Mississippi Mustard BBQ Sauce

My grandfather and my dad, Eli and Eli II, from Grenada, Mississippi, taught me this recipe. It is easy, simple and full of flavor.

1 cup mustard

½ cup ketchup

2 tablespoons honey

¼ cup hot sauce

¼ cup finely minced onion

Dash lemon juice

3 tablespoons cola (not diet)

Mix all together and simmer until onion is soft. Remove from heat and thin with additional cola if needed. Use as a sauce or for basting.

Cola Barbecue Sauce

1½ cups cola (not diet)

1½ cups ketchup

5 tablespoons Worcestershire sauce

5 tablespoons A-1 steak sauce

½ tablespoon liquid smoke

2 tablespoons chopped onion

½ tablespoon minced garlic

2 teaspoons black pepper

Hot sauce to taste

Combine all ingredients in a saucepan and boil 1 to 2 minutes. Reduce heat to low and simmer 10 to 15 minutes to thicken. Serve warm or cool completely before storing in fridge. I use a mason/canning jar for storing up to a week.

Tailgate Friendly

Tennessee Whiskey Brown Sugar Barbecue Sauce

½ cup Tennessee whiskey

⅓ cup brown sugar

1 small onion, finely diced

3 garlic cloves, minced

2 cups ketchup

¼ cup apple cider vinegar

2 tablespoons steak sauce

¼ cup Worcestershire sauce

1 tablespoon liquid smoke

½ tablespoon hot sauce

½ teaspoon pepper

½ teaspoon salt

In a medium saucepan, combine ingredients and simmer 20 minutes. Cool slightly and use as-is or purée in food processor or blender.

Something Extra

Alabama White Barbecue Sauce

This sauce is great on smoked chicken and turkey but also does wonders for pork and beef.

2 cups mayonnaise

½ cup apple cider vinegar

2 tablespoons lemon juice

1 tablespoon Worcestershire sauce

2 teaspoons ground black pepper

1 teaspoon salt

1 teaspoon cayenne pepper

1 to 2 teaspoons horseradish

Combine in a bowl, cover and chill before serving. You can add additional apple cider vinegar for a thinner sauce with a bit more bite.

Spicy White Alabama Barbecue Sauce

This version of white barbecue sauce is great on poultry and seafood. The sour cream makes a nice creamy texture.

1½ cups mayonnaise

½ cup sour cream

¼ cup apple cider vinegar

¼ cup ketchup

1 tablespoon hot sauce

1 tablespoon Worcestershire sauce

½ teaspoon each: salt and pepper

1 teaspoon cayenne pepper

Combine in a bowl, cover and chill before serving.

Carolina Vinegar Sauce

2 cups apple cider vinegar

2 tablespoons dark brown sugar

2 tablespoons ketchup

1½ tablespoons hot sauce

2 teaspoons red pepper flakes

2 teaspoons ground black
    pepper

1 teaspoon salt

Combine all ingredients in a saucepan and cook over medium-low heat about 20 minutes. Remove from heat and allow to cool before storing in fridge. Refrigerate 1 to 2 days before using, as flavors will really kick in.

Tangy Orange Juice Barbecue Sauce

My go-to meat choice for this sauce is chicken thighs.

2 to 3 tablespoons vegetable oil

⅔ cup chopped onion

⅓ cup chopped green bell
    pepper

1 tablespoon minced garlic

¾ cup orange juice

1 (8-ounce) can tomato sauce

¼ cup ketchup

⅓ cup brown sugar

2 tablespoons steak sauce

1 tablespoon apple cider
    vinegar

1 tablespoon Worcestershire
    sauce

Salt and pepper to taste

In a saucepan, heat vegetable oil over medium-high heat. Add onions, bell pepper and garlic; sauté about 2 minutes or until onion is opaque and bell pepper is soft.

Add remaining ingredients and bring to a boil. Reduce heat to low and simmer, uncovered, about 15 minutes.

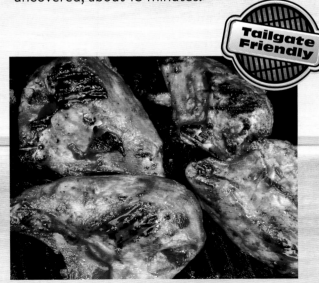

Tailgate Friendly

Something Extra

Thick and Saucy Barbecue Sauce

1 cup apple cider vinegar

1 cup ketchup

½ cup water

⅓ cup finely chopped onion

2 tablespoons minced garlic

2 tablespoons butter

2 tablespoons molasses (or 1 tablespoon maple syrup)

2 tablespoons mustard

2 tablespoons brown sugar

2 tablespoons Worcestershire sauce

½ tablespoon chili powder

Salt and pepper to taste

Combine all ingredients in a saucepan and cook over medium-low heat about 20 minutes. Remove from heat and cool before storing in fridge. Run this sauce through a blender if you want to liquefy the onions.

Barbecue Relish

1½ cups barbecue sauce

½ cup chopped tomato

½ cup chopped onion

½ cup chopped green or red bell pepper

¼ cup bacon bits

1 tablespoon balsamic vinegar

½ tablespoon minced garlic

¼ tablespoon dried cilantro

2 teaspoons Worcestershire sauce

2 teaspoons liquid smoke

Combine all ingredients in a saucepan and simmer over medium-low heat about 5 minutes. Use immediately or cool then refrigerate in a covered container.

Pale Ale Beer Mop Sauce

1 (12-ounce) bottle pale ale
  beer

⅓ cup apple cider vinegar

1½ tablespoons garlic powder

1 tablespoon onion powder

1 tablespoon sugar

1 tablespoon Worcestershire
  sauce

Combine all ingredients in a nonreactive
bowl and mix until sugar is dissolved. Use
as a mop sauce during offset grilling or
smoking.

Red Wine and Vinegar Beef Mop Sauce

1 cup red wine

½ cup red wine vinegar

¼ cup water

1 tablespoon garlic powder

2 teaspoons chili powder

2 teaspoons minced garlic

2 teaspoons Italian seasoning

Combine all ingredients in a bowl and mix
well. Use as a baste to keep grilled foods
moist while grilling.

Something Extra

Simple Steak Sauce

One of my first restaurant cooking jobs taught me the beauty of simplicity. The head chef would take chopped onions, ketchup and Worcestershire sauce, simmer them in a saucepan and we'd have a saucepan of the house steak sauce. This recipe has a few more ingredients but it's still simple.... And really good.

1 cup ketchup

⅓ cup Worcestershire sauce

2 tablespoons vinegar

1 tablespoon soy sauce

1 tablespoon onion powder

½ tablespoon minced garlic

2 teaspoons lemon juice

2 teaspoons mustard

Dash salt and pepper

Combine all ingredients in a saucepan and cover. Simmer over medium-low heat about 10 minutes. Serve warm or cool completely before covering and placing in your refrigerator.

Tzatziki Sauce

Tzatziki is a popular dip, topping and spread in many back yards during grilling season.

1 cup plain Greek yogurt

2 to 3 tablespoons peeled and finely chopped cucumber

1 tablespoon lemon juice

1 tablespoon olive oil

½ tablespoon minced garlic

½ tablespoon dill

½ teaspoon salt

½ teaspoon pepper

Dash parsley flakes (fresh if possible)

Combine all ingredients in a bowl and mix well. Refrigerate and serve cold.

Easy Steak Sauce Butter

Butter makes a great steak sauce. Try this amped-up butter the next time you toss a few steaks on the grill.

1 stick butter or margarine, softened

1 tablespoon steak sauce

2 teaspoons minced garlic

½ teaspoon black pepper

½ teaspoon sugar

Mix all ingredients well; chill to set. If desired, roll in wax paper for a tube shape that you can slice. Spread on your steak just before removing from grill or while steaks rest. Save in a covered container in fridge up to a week.

Easy Italian Herb Steak Butter

1 stick butter or margarine, softened

1 tablespoon Italian seasoning

2 teaspoons parsley

Mix all ingredients well; chill to set. If desired, roll in wax paper for a tube shape that you can slice. Spread on your steak just before removing from grill or while steaks rest. Save in a covered container in fridge up to a week.

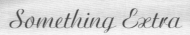

Something Extra

Avocado Mayonnaise

½ cup mayonnaise

½ avocado, peeled, pitted and mashed

½ tablespoon lemon juice

1 teaspoon garlic powder

Dash salt and pepper

Combine all ingredients in a bowl. Cover and chill before using.

Chipotle Mayo

1 cup mayonnaise

2 chipotle peppers in adobo sauce

1 tablespoon adobo sauce

½ tablespoon lime juice

2 teaspoons chile pepper

Salt and pepper to taste

Combine all ingredients in a food processor and pulse on low until smooth.

Bacon Mayo

This mayonnaise is perfect for burgers or BLT sandwiches. My tip: when you cook bacon for breakfast, simply save a few spoonfuls of grease and a couple strips of bacon.

1 cup mayonnaise

3 to 4 bacon strips, cooked and finely crumbled

1 tablespoon bacon grease

Combine all of the ingredients in a bowl and mix.

SUPER SIDES

FLIP THOSE CHIPS! A bag of chips and some dip can be considered a side dish and those will certainly do in a pinch. Today's grill masters often dedicate an equal amount of time to fantastic side dishes as to the main dish. One thing is for sure, your guests will appreciate the extra effort.

There are so many great side options and so many variations of each, I could have written a whole other book just on that. Of course, this IS a grilling cookbook. So, here is a short selection of just a few of my favorite side dishes.

Something Extra

Bacon Mac and Cheese

Macaroni and cheese is a classic side dish for any cookout. This version just happens to be loaded up with a few extras.

3 cups elbow macaroni (or shells)

1½ sticks butter, divided

¼ cup self-rising flour

1 cup milk

½ pound Velveeta, cut into chunks

1 cup shredded Cheddar cheese

1 cup cooked and crumbled bacon

Salt and pepper to taste

¼ cup crushed Ritz crackers

Cook macaroni per package directions but do not cook fully. Drain and set aside.

In a large skillet over medium heat, melt half the butter; add flour and mix well. Add milk slowly, mixing well. Add Velveeta and Cheddar cheese; cook and stir until melted and everything is well combined.

Treat a heavy-duty foil pan with nonstick spray. Combine macaroni, cheese sauce, and bacon. Season to taste with salt and pepper. Place mixture in foil pan.

Melt remaining butter in a bowl in microwave. Stir in cracker crumbs and spoon evenly over macaroni. Cover with foil and place on upper rack of a covered grill using medium-high to high heat. Close grill lid and cook 35 to 40 minutes or until macaroni is full cooked.

Remove foil about 5 minutes before done.

TO BAKE INDOORS:
You can bake in a 350° preheated oven about 30 minutes or until cracker topping is golden brown.

Kent's Creamy Buttermilk Coleslaw

This recipe is my favorite for serving up with everything from pulled pork barbecue and hot dogs to southern-style fried chicken. You can't go wrong if you make it in bulk for a large crowd such as a golf tournament or tailgate party.

8 cups finely chopped cabbage

½ to ⅔ cup finely chopped carrots

2 tablespoons finely chopped onion

½ cup mayonnaise

¼ cup buttermilk

¼ cup milk

⅓ cup sugar

1 teaspoon salt

1 teaspoon pepper

1½ tablespoons white vinegar

2 tablespoons lemon juice

Mix everything in a large bowl and stir to mix well. Cover and chill in refrigerator about an hour before serving.

Something Extra

Carolina Vinegar Slaw

Be sure to allow an hour or more for the slaw to chill. That way the flavors really combine.

1 head cabbage, shredded

1 bell pepper, thinly sliced

½ sweet onion, thinly sliced

1 to 2 carrots, shredded or
    chopped

1½ cups apple cider vinegar

½ cup water

2 tablespoons oil

⅓ cup sugar

Crushed red pepper to taste

Salt and pepper to taste

Combine ingredients in a bowl, cover and chill for an hour or longer. Toss gently before serving.

Hearty Three-Bean Baked Beans

1 large onion, finely chopped

1 tablespoon minced garlic

¼ cup extra virgin olive oil

1 (15-ounce) can pork and beans

1 (15-ounce) can kidney beans

1 (15-ounce) can black beans

½ cup finely diced tomatoes

¼ cup brown sugar

¼ cup beer

6 to 8 bacon strips

In a skillet, sauté onion and garlic in olive oil.

Pour pork and beans into a glass baking dish; add sautéed onion and garlic.

Drain and rinse kidney beans and black beans; add to dish. Add tomatoes, brown sugar and beer. Mix well and cover loosely with foil.

Bake at 250° for 1½ hours. Uncover and lay bacon strips on top. Return to oven (uncovered) and bake an additional hour.

Something Extra

Presidential Prairie Baked Beans

President Herbert Hoover was known for his food relief programs following World War II, long after he had left office. His efforts included educating the American public on food conservation to help with the war effort. Beans were a large part of the solution in feeding masses of hungry people. We can thank him for popularizing "Meatless Mondays" as part of a wartime effort to conserve.

1 pound navy beans

2 medium onions, diced

½ cup molasses

¼ cup brown sugar

1 teaspoon salt

1 teaspoon dry mustard

1 cup boiling water

¼ pound salt pork, scored to the rind

Rinse beans and soak overnight in water to cover.

Drain and place beans in large saucepan; cover with water. Add onions and simmer 1 hour or until tender. Drain and pour into a 2-quart bean pot or casserole.

Combine molasses, brown sugar, salt and dry mustard. Add boiling water; mix well. Pour over beans. Place salt pork on top.

Cover and bake at 300° for 5 hours, adding water if top seems dry. Uncover and bake 1 more hour. Serve hot.

Gone Fishing: Hoover was also a lifelong avid fisherman and outdoorsman who proudly proclaimed, "Man and boy, the American is a fisherman. That comprehensive list of human rights, the Declaration of Independence, is firm that all men (and boys) are endowed with certain inalienable rights, including life, liberty, and the pursuit of happiness, which obviously includes the pursuit of...fish."

Tex-Mex Cast Iron Trail Beans

A wagon train cook's version of cleaning out the fridge.

1 tablespoon olive oil

1 jalapeño, diced

1 small red bell pepper, diced

½ onion, chopped

2 garlic cloves, minced

2 (15-ounce) cans pork and beans

1 (15-ounce) can whole-kernel corn

1 (10-ounce) can Rotel tomatoes

1 beef bouillon cube

1 tablespoon cumin

1 tablespoon chili powder

½ tablespoon hot sauce

1 tablespoon apple vinegar

Water as needed

Heat oil in a large cast-iron pot over charcoal; add the jalapeños, bell peppers, onion and garlic. Cook and stir until browned.

Stir in remaining ingredients. Cover and cook an hour, stirring as needed. Add water as needed.

Move to cooler coals if sticking or cooking too quickly.

OVEN METHOD:

Heat oil in a skillet; add the jalapeños, bell peppers, onion and garlic. Cook and stir until browned.

Combine with remaining ingredients in an oven-safe cast-iron pot (or baking dish with a lid). Cover and bake at 300° about 3 hours. May be done at 2 hours but the extra bake time will enhance the flavor.

WHO INVENTED THE CHARCOAL BRIQUETTE?

Many people think Henry Ford invented the charcoal briquette when wood scraps from his car production were combined with coal and binders in 1920. In fact, Ellsworth B. A. Zwoyer of Pennsylvania patented a charcoal briquette design years prior in 1897. Following World War One, Zwoyer's company, aptly named Zwoyer Fuel Company, built plants in Buffalo, New York and Fall River, Massachusetts.

Something Extra

Hot German Potato Salad with Eggs

Every year, my wife Ally and I travel to Helen, Georgia, for the annual Oktoberfest celebration where we drink our fair share of assorted brewed beverages and eat too much food, including delicious German potato salad.

About 12 red potatoes, sliced

8 slices bacon, cooked and crumbled

1 medium red onion, chopped

1 tablespoon all-purpose flour

½ cup water

¼ cup beer

2 tablespoons vinegar

1 tablespoon sugar

1 tablespoon mustard

½ teaspoon salt

⅛ teaspoon pepper

¼ cup chopped celery

2 hard-boiled eggs, chopped

Parsley flakes

Boil potatoes in water to cover until just tender.

While potatoes cook, fry bacon in a skillet. Remove bacon to cool and sauté onion in drippings.

Remove skillet from heat (to avoid splashing hot bacon grease on hot stove when adding liquid) and carefully add flour, water, beer and vinegar. Stir to mix and add remaining ingredients, except eggs and parsley.

When potatoes are done, drain well. Combine potatoes and sauce in a large glass bowl. Stir in eggs and parsley flakes. Serve warm.

AMERICANS LOVE POTATOES!

The average American eats more than 130 pounds of potatoes a year. The leading brand of frozen potatoes in the U.S. is Ore-Ida, a member of the Heinz family of brands since 1963. Americans buy about 1 billion pounds of Ore-Ida potatoes a year.

Source: Heinz

Something Extra

Bacon & Ranch Potato Salad

12 to 14 small red potatoes

½ cup ranch dressing

¼ cup sour cream

½ cup shredded Cheddar cheese

1 cup cooked and crumbled bacon

½ cup chopped celery

1 small sweet onion, finely chopped

1 teaspoon garlic powder

Dash crushed red pepper flakes

Salt and pepper to taste

Wash potatoes and dice (with the skin on) into small pieces. Boil until just tender but not fully cooked. (You're not making mashed potatoes.) Remove from heat, drain and place in a bowl to cool.

Combine remaining ingredients and mix well. Pour over potatoes and stir gently to mix; cover and cool before serving.

Cajun Grilled Potatoes Bites

This recipe is perfect for any type potato. I like small red potatoes, but you can use russet, sweet or any combination. The trick is to cube the potatoes into equal-size cubes to allow for even cooking on the grill.

1 pound small red potatoes

½ sweet onion, finely diced

Olive oil (or vegetable oil)

Cajun seasoning to taste

Red pepper flakes to taste

Rinse potatoes and dice into equal-sized ½-inch pieces. In a bowl, combine potatoes with remaining ingredients, tossing gently to evenly coat.

Place in a treated foil pan and cover with foil. Place on grill over high heat. Cooking time will be at least 20 to 30 minutes so I throw them on the grill ahead my meats.

Once potatoes are cooked through, remove foil and cook another 5 minutes.

How to Cook Corn on the Cob in a Cooler

I love this recipe! Actually, it's more method than recipe. Don't use a huge cooler – you don't need a massive, truck-bed-sized cooler to cook 12 pieces of corn. Don't use a broken, old or dingy cooler. Use a clean cooler that seals properly to keep the heat inside. Unless you have a cooler that you can dedicate to cooking corn, then avoid melted butter or seasoning. I can tell you from experience that melted butter is tough to remove from a cooler. You might want to place a sign on the corn cooler pointing your guests to the beer cooler so the lid does not get opened early.

12 ears corn, shucked

2 to 3 tea kettles boiling water (enough to cover corn without overflowing cooler)

Butter, optional

Salt to taste, optional

Place all ingredients in cooler, close the lid and wait 30 minutes (don't peek). Carefully open cooler to vent heat before removing corn. Serve hot.

WHO INVENTED THE PORTABLE PICNIC COOLER?

Coolers have been around a long time in the form of stand-alone ice chests for the kitchen, coolers for military use, and more. But when it comes to the portable cooler design we know today, we can thank Richard Laramy who patented his consumer-friendly invention in 1953. Laramy's design was made famous shortly afterwards by the Coleman Company.

Something Extra

Fried Green Tomatoes with Barbecue Cream Sauce

These Fried Green Tomatoes are great by themselves or add to hamburgers, BLTs or on a grilled ham and cheese sandwich. Yum.

3 to 4 green tomatoes, sliced ½ inch thick

2 eggs, beaten

½ cup cornmeal

Salt and pepper to taste

Dash Creole (or Cajun) seasoning to taste

Oil for frying

BARBECUE CREAM SAUCE:

1 cup barbecue sauce

½ cup sour cream

Set tomatoes aside. Beat eggs in a small bowl. In a shallow dish, combine cornmeal, salt, pepper and Creole seasoning. Heat oil in a skillet over medium-high heat. Dip tomato slices, 1 at a time, in egg then cover in cornmeal mixture. Fry in hot oil until golden brown.

For Sauce: In a bowl, combine barbecue sauce with sour cream and mix well. Drizzle over Fried Green Tomatoes or serve on the side for dipping.

Grilled Summer Squash with Almond Pesto Sauce

2 to 3 medium squash

Olive oil

Salt and pepper to taste

Garlic powder to taste

Grated Parmesan cheese to taste

ALMOND PESTO:

¼ cup plain almonds

1 tablespoon minced garlic

2 cups chopped fresh basil

½ cup olive oil

Small dash nutmeg

Salt and pepper to taste

Rinse and slice squash, leaving the skin on. (You can slice into nice round pieces or slice lengthwise if you have smaller squash.) Brush squash with olive oil; sprinkle with salt, pepper, garlic powder and cheese.

Grill over medium-high heat until grill marks appear and edges are golden, about 6 minutes. Serve hot topped with Pesto.

For Pesto: Preheat oven to 400° and toast almonds on a cookie sheet for 8 to 10 minutes. Remove from oven and cool completely.

Combine toasted almonds with garlic, basil, olive oil, nutmeg, salt and pepper in a food processor. Process until a nice paste is formed. Add a few additional drips of olive oil if too thick.

Grilled Zucchini Slices

2 large zucchini (select wide ones)

Olive oil

Garlic powder to taste

Grated Parmesan cheese, to taste

Slice zucchini into ¼-inch pieces and brush with olive oil. (Wider zucchini make for wider slices with more area for toppings.) Sprinkle with garlic powder and Parmesan cheese.

Grill over medium-high heat 5 to 6 minutes, turning once about halfway through.

MAKE IT A ZUCCHINI PIZZA:
Why not turn your Grilled Zucchini Slices into a mini pizza? After grilling one side, load it up with your favorite pizza toppings and return to the grill to cook the bottom and melt the cheese. The combinations are endless — let your foodie imagination go wild.

Simple Southern Succotash

2 tablespoons vegetable oil

1 (16-ounce) package
frozen lima beans

1 (16-ounce) package
frozen whole-kernel corn

Salt and pepper to taste

2 tomatoes, chopped

⅔ cup chopped sweet
onion

¼ cup butter

Place oil in a large saucepan; add beans and corn. Cook over medium-low heat, covered, until thawed. Add salt and pepper, tomato and onion; cover and cook until onion is soft, stirring as needed. Stir in butter and cook until melted. Serve hot.

(You can use frozen, canned or fresh veggies. The key is having equal amounts of beans and corn kernels.)

Three Ways to Serve Southern Succotash

Simple Southern Succotash is great right out of a bowl, but here are three more ways to serve it.

- **Appetizer Succotash Bruschetta:** Yes I know that bruschetta is an Italian dish using grilled bread, olive oil and a growing list of toppings, including the barbecue version in this book. So, since the door's open on toppings, why not try your next homemade bruschetta topped with succotash?

- **Mini Succotash Puffs:** I've had succotash served in a pie shell several times. So, I figured why not make them smaller and serve as an appetizer? Spoon Simple Southern Succotash into mini puff pastry shells or mini pie crusts. Serve hot or cold.

- **Barbecue Succotash Salad:** Use cold ingredients such as canned and drained corn, lima beans, additional beans, plus chopped onions, colored bell peppers, and seasoning. Stir in a few spoonfuls of barbecues sauce, cover, chill and serve.

Something Extra

What the Heck Is Succotash?

Here in the South, we proudly declare any dish that combines corn and lima beans with a few other veggies as being "Succotash." Recipes vary slightly from region to region on ingredients, as well as the way it's served - salad, side dish or casserole. Food historians will tell you the dish was very popular during the Great Depression due to low cost and ease of cooking. Before that, it's believed Native Americans of the northeastern woodlands were the first to prepare versions of the dish. All I know is..."Sufferin' succotash" is a catchphrase used by several of my favorite cartoon characters!

Sweet Broccoli Salad

I'm a bit of a broccoli salad freak. It's an easy dish that can be made a variety of ways. Plus, it's always a crowd pleaser.

3 cups broccoli florets

1 cup finely chopped broccoli stems

½ cup shredded carrots

¼ cup finely chopped sweet onion

¼ cup golden raisins

½ cup shredded cheese

2 tablespoons real bacon bits

½ cup mayonnaise

1 tablespoon sugar

½ tablespoon apple cider vinegar

Combine all ingredients in a bowl, cover and chill before serving.

THE BAGGED BROCCOLI SLAW VERSION:

Use recipe above substituting broccoli with packaged broccoli slaw from the produce department at your local grocery store.

CORNBREAD BROCCOLI SALAD:

Same as Sweet Broccoli Salad but with a heaping cup cooked and crumbled cornbread added (perfect for using your leftover cornbread).

BACON BROCCOLI SALAD:

Same as Sweet Broccoli Salad but with a cup of crumbled cooked bacon added in place of bacon bits.

Something Extra

Cornbread Salad

There's not a piece of lettuce anywhere near this recipe but somebody decided to term it "salad." To them, I am thankful.

2 (8.5-ounce) boxes cornbread mix, plus ingredients to prepare per package directions

2 to 3 red tomatoes, diced

2 to 3 green bell peppers, diced

1 red onion, diced

1 cup cooked and crumbled bacon

¼ cup sugar

½ cup mayonnaise

½ cup ranch dressing

Milk to thin

Shredded Cheddar cheese

Bake cornbread as directed on box. Cool and break into large pieces in a bowl. (Don't over-crumble as pieces will break down more when mixing salad.)

Add tomatoes, bell peppers, onion and bacon; gently mix.

In a separate bowl, combine sugar, mayonnaise and ranch dressing. Add a dash of milk if mixture is too thick. (You want it to pour like a thick milkshake.)

Combine dressing mixture with cornbread mixture; cover and chill 10 to 15 minutes before serving. Just before serving, sprinkle with cheese.

Super Sides

DELECTABLE DESSERTS

What better way to finish off a great grilling session than with some tasty desserts? Here are just a few of my favorite desserts to serve after a delicious meal off the grill. A couple of them can even be cooked on the grill.

Something Extra

Tennessee Whiskey Pecan Pie

1 (8-inch) pie shell

4 eggs, beaten

1 cup brown sugar

¾ cup maple syrup

1 tablespoon bourbon

3 tablespoons butter, melted

1 cup chopped pecans

Preheat oven to 400° and bake pie shell about 5 minutes or until lightly brown.

Mix eggs, sugar, syrup, bourbon and butter together and beat well.

Spread pecans in prebaked pie shell. Slowly pour sugar mixture on top.

Bake about 30 minutes at 400°; reduce heat to 300° and bake another 45 minutes. Reduce oven to 200° and cook an additional 30 minutes or until pie is firm in the center and pecans are cooked to a golden brown.

Icebox Peanut Butter Pie

4 ounces cream cheese, softened

1 cup powdered sugar

8 ounces Cool Whip

¾ cup peanut butter

1 (9-inch) graham cracker pie crust

CHOCOLATE GLAZE:

¼ cup chocolate chips

¼ cup whipping cream, whipped

1 teaspoon corn syrup

Whip cream cheese until fluffy. Add powdered sugar and mix well. Fold in Cool Whip and peanut butter; blend well. Spoon mixture into crust and smooth top as flat as possible. Freeze while making Chocolate Glaze.

For Glaze: In a small saucepan over low heat, melt chocolate chips. Stir in whipped cream and corn syrup. Stir until smooth; remove from heat. Pour over pie. Refrigerate at least 2 hours before serving.

Double Crust Pie Crusts from Scratch

Chill the shortening and butter and use ice cold water for best results.

3 cups all-purpose flour

2½ teaspoons sugar

¾ teaspoon salt

⅔ cup vegetable shortening, chilled and cut into pieces

10 tablespoons (1¼ sticks) unsalted butter, chilled and cut into small pieces

10 tablespoons ice water

Combine flour, sugar and salt in a bowl. Add shortening and butter, a little at a time. Cut with a fork until you have a dry coarse-looking mixture.

Add ice water, 3 tablespoons at a time, and mix until well moistened and dough clings together (but is not wet).

Shape into a ball and cut in half. Wrap each half tightly in cling wrap and refrigerate an hour or longer.

When you're ready to make your pie, simply unwrap dough and roll out each one on a floured surface to fit a 9-inch pie dish.

Something Extra

Ally's Apple Cider Apple Pie

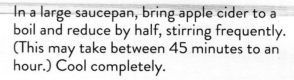

Here's one of my favorite recipes from Ally's apple pie collection.

1¾ cups apple cider

8 apples, peeled, cored and sliced

1 tablespoon lemon juice

⅔ cup sugar

2 tablespoons flour

1 teaspoon cinnamon

2 Double Crust Pie Crusts from Scratch (page 272)

⅓ stick butter, melted

1 tablespoon sugar

¼ tablespoon brown sugar

In a large saucepan, bring apple cider to a boil and reduce by half, stirring frequently. (This may take between 45 minutes to an hour.) Cool completely.

Preheat oven to 375°. While reduced cider is cooling, place apples and lemon juice in a large bowl.

In a small bowl, combine sugar, flour and cinnamon; add to apples. Toss or use a spoon to gently coat apples.

Place 1 pie crust into a glass pie dish coated with a flour-based nonstick spray. Spoon apples into pie crust and pour cooled cider over top.

Cover with 2nd pie crust and pinch edges with bottom crust to seal. Use a knife to make several small slices in top the crust to release steam. Brush with melted butter and sprinkle with sugar and brown sugar. Bake 45 minutes and check apples for doneness.

Depending on your oven, and the amount the cider reduced, you may need to bake another 10 minutes or so. You may also need to wrap the edges of the crust in foil so they won't burn. Allow pie to cool an hour before serving.

Grilled Buttered Honey Rum Bananas

2 tablespoons rum

2 tablespoons honey

1 tablespoon melted butter

4 firm bananas

Cinnamon to taste

Brown sugar to taste

Ice cream

Combine rum, honey and melted butter in a bowl and mix well.

Preheat grill to medium-high and treat grates with nonstick spray. Peel bananas and slice lengthwise.

Place bananas on a grill and baste generously with rum mixture. Sprinkle with cinnamon and brown sugar. Grill 5 minutes or less, just long enough to caramelize sauce.

Serve hot topped with ice cream.

Something Extra

Grilled Pound Cake

I've grilled pizza. Why not cake? Actually, Grilled Pound Cake is my signature dessert. You can make your own pound cake and ice cream from scratch or you can save some time and pick some up at the store.

Cooking spray, for grill

4 slices pound cake

Spray butter

2 to 3 teaspoons brown sugar, optional

4 scoops ice cream

1 cup sliced strawberries

¼ cup strawberry syrup

⅓ cup toasted and sliced almonds

Preheat grill to medium heat. Coat grill grates (or foil or grill basket) with cooking spray.

Coat cake slice with spray butter. Grill until edges are browned and cake is hot. If desired, sprinkle with brown sugar before removing from grill.

Place 1 slice on each plate and top with ice cream, sliced strawberries, strawberry syrup and almonds.

Something Extra

Country Cola Cake

Chattanooga, Tennessee, has deep roots when it comes to cola. It was home to the first Coca-Cola bottling plant and is also the home of Double Cola, which was born around 1922 and has been a staple around the South ever since.

CAKE:

2 cups all-purpose flour

2 cups sugar

3 tablespoons cocoa

1 cup Double Cola

1 cup butter

1½ cups miniature marshmallows

2 eggs, beaten

½ cup buttermilk

1 teaspoon baking soda

1 teaspoon vanilla extract

FROSTING:

½ cup butter

1 tablespoon cocoa

6 tablespoons Double Cola

1 (1-pound) box powdered sugar

½ cup chopped pecans

Grease and flour a 9x13-inch pan and set aside. In a large bowl, combine flour and sugar.

In a medium-size saucepan, combine cocoa, Double Cola, butter and marshmallows; bring to a slow boil. Add to flour mixture and mix well. Mix in eggs, buttermilk, baking soda and vanilla and mix well.

Pour batter into prepared pan and bake at 350° for 35 to 40 minutes, until cake tests done. Remove from oven and cool while preparing Frosting.

For Frosting: In a saucepan, bring butter, cocoa and Double Cola to a boil. Stir in sugar and mix well. Remove from heat and stir in nuts.

Use the round end of a small wooden spoon to poke holes in cake every 2 inches. Before the Frosting cools, pour over cake.

INDEX

Great American Grilling

Great American Grilling

Index

Index

ABOUT THE AUTHOR

Kent "The Deck Chef" Whitaker has taken his down-home, Southern-style cooking to an art-form. "I like to do a bit more than burgers and dogs on the grill."

He has appeared on the Food Network and other network television stations and is the winner of the Emeril Live / Food Network barbecue contest. He frequently hosts cooking classes throughout the South as well as numerous book signings and chef demos. He hosts a short-format cooking radio show which is heard on more than 60 affiliates nationwide and writes monthly articles for *The National Barbecue News* and other publications.

Kent is also a sports writer regularly covering NASCAR, ARCA Racing, INDYCAR racing, and occasionally the NFL. All of which include...you guessed it, grilling and tailgating.

He is co-editor of the *State Hometown Cookbook Series* (Great American Publishers.) He is also the author of *Smoke in the Mountains* and *Checkered Flag Cooking* (Quail Ridge Press), and has written and illustrated two children's books, *Why are the Mountains Smoky?* (Overmountain Press) and *Big Mo's Tennis Ball Hunt* (Great American Publishers). He has also written three history books, *The USS Alabama* (Arcadia Publishing), *Talladega Superspeedway* (Arcadia Publishing) and *Bullets and Bread: Feeding the Troops in World War Two* (History Publishing Company).

Kent and his wife Ally live in East Tennessee and are the proud ARMY Strong parents of Macee Whitaker as well as members of the United States Coast Guard Auxiliary. Their grilling sessions include family, friends, a Golden Retriever named Moses, a Presa-Canario named King, and a Shitzu named Lucy.

State Hometown Cookbook Series

A Hometown Taste of America, One State at a Time.

Each state's hometown charm is revealed through local recipes from real hometown cooks along with stories and photos that will take you back to your hometown . . . or take you on a journey to explore other hometowns across the country.

EACH: $18.95 • 240 to 272 pages • 8x9 • paperbound
**Alabama • Georgia • Louisiana • Mississippi
South Carolina • Tennessee • Texas • West Virginia**

Eat & Explore Cookbook Series

Discover community celebrations and unique destinations, as they share their favorite recipes.

Experience our United States like never before when you explore the distinct flavor of each state by savoring 250 favorite recipes from the state's best cooks. In addition, the state's favorite events and destinations are profiled throughout the book with fun stories and everything you need to know to plan your family's next road trip.

EACH: $18.95 • 240 to 272 pages • 7x9 • paperbound

**Arkansas • Minnesota • North Carolina
Ohio • Oklahoma • Virginia • Washington**

State Back Road Restaurants Series

Every road leads to delicious food.

From two-lane highways and interstates, to dirt roads and quaint downtowns, every road leads to delicious food when traveling across our United States. The STATE BACK ROAD RESTAURANTS COOKBOOK SERIES serves up a well-researched and charming guide to each state's best back road restaurants. No time to travel? No problem. Each restaurant shares with you their favorite recipes—sometimes their signature dish, sometimes a family favorite, but always delicious.

EACH: $18.95 • 256 pages • 7x9 • paperbound

Alabama • Kentucky • Tennessee • Texas

---

www.GreatAmericanPublishers.com • www.facebook.com/GreatAmericanPublishers

It's So Easy to Cook Food Your Family will Love

Easy-to-afford, easy-to-prepare recipes for feeding your family

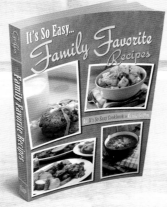

Family Favorite Recipes
is a collection of recipes handed down through generations of outstanding cooks. You will find easy recipes using ingredients you probably already have on hand so you can feed your family fast…and deliciously.

256 pages • $18.95
7x10 • paperbound

Kitchen Memories Cookbook
is a cookbook, memory book, and activity book—all in one—making it so easy to spend time with your family making fun kitchen memories of your own.

256 pages • $18.95
7x10 • paperbound

Great American Grilling
offers up easy-to-follow recipes and methods for grilling, smoking, outdoor cooking, and tailgating. The ultimate grill guide simple enough for the beginner and fun for the everyday outdoor cook.

288 pages • $21.95
7x10 • paperbound

www.GreatAmericanPublishers.com • www.facebook.com/GreatAmericanPublishers

- -

ORDER FORM

Mail to: Great American Publishers • 501 Avalon Way, Suite B • Brandon, MS 39047
Or call us toll-free 1.888.854.5954 to order by check or credit card.

❑ Check Enclosed

Charge to: ❑ Visa ❑ MC ❑ AmEx ❑ Disc

Card#_____

Exp Date _____

Signature_____

Name_____

Address _____

City _____ State _____ Zip _____

Phone_____

Email_____

QTY. TITLE   TOTAL

_____ ____

_____ ____

_____ ____

_____ ____

_____ ____

Subtotal _____

Postage ($4 first book; $1 each additional) _____
Order 5 or more books, get FREE shipping

Total _____

288